FAMILY
IN
MENDIP,
AVALON,
& SEDGEMOOR

Nigel Vile

Scarthin Books, Cromford, Derbyshire   1991

A

i

FAMILY WALKS
IN MENDIP, AVALON & SEDGEMOOR

Family Walks Series
General Editor: Norman Taylor

———————

THE COUNTRY CODE
Enjoy the countryside and respect its life and work
Guard against all risk of fire
Fasten all gates
Keep your dogs under close control
Keep to public paths across farmland
Use gates and stiles to cross fences, hedges and walls
Leave livestock, crops and machinery alone
Take your litter home
Help to keep all water clean
Protect wildlife, plants and trees
Take special care on country roads
Make no unnecessary noise

———————

Published 1991

Phototypesetting, printing by Higham Press Ltd., Shirland, Derbyshire

ISBN 0 907758 41 X

THE RIVER BRUE, BALTONSBOROUGH (Route 11)

1

Preface

The pressure that mass tourism is placing upon our heritage is a concern that extends far beyond the boundaries of the Green movement. 'Tourist pollution' is already at such a level in some localities that the more thoughtful visitors are beginning to vote with their feet. We are in danger of killing the proverbial goose that lays the golden egg. Thoughts like these were passing through my mind as I drove through Cheddar Gorge one fine summer's morning. Already the crowds on the pavements were four-deep and spilling into the road, bringing passing traffic to a standstill. All the while, mind-numbing muzak was issuing forth from the many gift-shops that lined both sides of the road. I actually began to question the wisdom of writing a guidebook like this that might add to the number of visitors to the area! Within minutes, however, I was heading across the Somerset Levels to Wedmore. I pulled into a field entrance to take a few photographs and looked back towards Cheddar. High above the gorge, where only footpaths and serious walkers penetrate, the landscape was virtually deserted. It once again seemed a positive project that I was working on. In the preparation of this volume, I often spent whole days in the field without meeting more than half-a-dozen fellow travellers. I commend this book to you as the perfect antidote for the discontented mien!

Acknowledgements

The sketches that accompany some of the walks were produced by my sister-in-law, Trisha Martyn, of Wednesbury in the West Midlands. Thanks Trisha! My thanks also go to my wife Gill, for creating the time and space for me to produce this book, and to my children - Laura, Katie and James - for being patient guinea-pigs!

About the Author

Nigel Vile currently teaches at King Edward's School in Bath. He was born in Bristol more years ago than he cares to remember, and currently lives in Bradford-on-Avon. As well as this book of rambles, he is also the author of companion volumes that cover Bath & Bristol and the County of Wiltshire. He is also a regular contributor to the 'Down Your Way' section of the "Country Walking' magazine.

CONTENTS

MAP OF THE AREA

Numbers (5 etc.) indicate start of walk

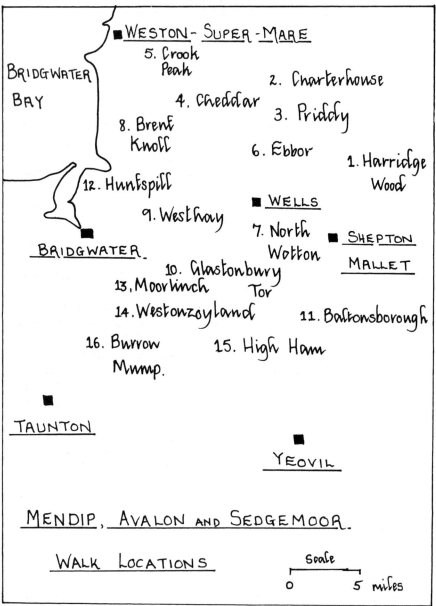

WESTON - SUPER - MARE

5. Crook Peak

2. Charterhouse

BRIDGWATER BAY

4. Cheddar

3. Priddy

8. Brent Knoll

6. Ebbor

1. Harridge Wood

12. Huntspill

WELLS

9. Westhay

7. North Wotton

SHEPTON MALLET

BRIDGWATER

10. Glastonbury Tor

13. Moorlinch

14. Westonzoyland

11. Baltonsborough

16. Burrow Mump.

15. High Ham

TAUNTON

YEOVIL

MENDIP, AVALON AND SEDGEMOOR.

WALK LOCATIONS

Scale

0   5 miles

Introduction

Welcome to this collection of walks written with the family very much in mind! Too many walking guides have routes that average out at between 5 and 10 miles in length, with quite severe gradients and rough terrain. This book, to quote a phrase, will hopefully prove to be "something completely different'. The length of each walk has been kept deliberately short, the average distance being 4 miles, in order that a normal fit youngster can complete the distance. As far as possible, you will find that a pub or tea-shop will either await you en-route, or at the end of a walk, failing which a choice of fine picnicking sites has been indicated. Road-walking has been kept to a minimum, although many of the walks criss-cross roads to facilitate the rescue of tired youngsters (or parents!) should the need arise. To add interest for youngsters, each walk contains a number of suitable attractions. It may be a small cave, possibly a shallow stream for paddling, or perhaps a traditional windmill. Finally, each route is circular to avoid any retracing of steps.

The corner of Somerset described in this book provides us with two fascinating environments. To the north, the first 7 circuits explore the Mendip Hills, a limestone upland rising to over 1,000 feet above sea-level. This is a landscape of pot-holes and caves, gorges and rock outcrops, with interest aplenty for the active youngster. In an earlier volume - 'Family Walks Around Bath and Bristol' - I took the opportunity to describe 4 circuits in the Mendip Hills. This clearly left a lot of ground uncovered, and in this new volume I have attempted to fill some of the gaps. Spread out to the south of the Mendips are the Somerset Levels, once a marshy wilderness where isolated hills like the Tor at Glastonbury formed lonely islands of human habitation. Running across the Levels are the Polden Hills, dividing the lowlands into Avalon to the north, and Sedgemoor to the south. History pervades the Levels. Legends and tales of King Arthur impregnate Glastonbury, and there is more concrete evidence of King Alfred at Burrow Mump. Drainage of the Levels by a complex network of channels and rhynes has left the area somewhat drier than formerly, although it still remains an ideal habitat for moisture-loving plants and animals. It is this curious and ancient landscape that this book of 'Family Walks' explores.

Choosing a walk

Never throw inexperienced youngsters "in at the deep end" when walking! Rutted tracks and slippery hillsides are far harder going than the pavements that lead to the manicured lawns of your local park. Routes 1,

5

PEAT CUTTING, WESTHAY (Route 9)

5, 8 and 10 make ideal introductory half-day rambles. On more strenuous routes, a good idea is to make contingency plans so that if the party gets part-way, and exhausted youngsters think that going to the dentist is preferable to walking, rescue can be arranged by meeting friends with transport at a suitable point, or by a driver hurrying back to collect the car. In the appendices, I have made a subjective assessment of the routes in order of difficulty, to help you choose.

Allowing sufficient time

Each walk is intended to take up the best part of a half or whole day, allowing time for play, exploration and rest. It is better to over-estimate the time required, thus avoiding the need to have to 'route march' the latter part of the journey. As a rough guide, allow a pace of around one mile per hour for very young children, graduating to two miles per hour for the experienced ten-year-old.

What to wear

It should go without saying that, given the British climate, it is advisable to go walking prepared for the worst! Proper walking-boots or stout shoes are preferable to wellington boots, which are fine for walking the dog in the park but are tiring and rub on more serious walks. Following a spell of dry weather, the quality of the drove tracks and bridlepaths in Somerset does make trainers a feasible option on the shorter walks. On top, I prefer several thin layers that can gradually be peeled off as it gets warmer, rather than one thick jumper that just gives the hot/cold options! Waterproof cagoules are a must, too. Cords are better than jeans, the latter being extremely uncomfortable when wet due to their 'clinginess'. A cap or bobble-hat is also useful during colder weather, bearing in mind that the crown of the head is where the body's greatest heat-loss will occur. Don't forget a small rucksack for all those items that made a walk that much more enjoyable - picnics, maps, cameras, spotter guides, towels and so on.

Route-finding

The maps in this book, taken in conjunction with the directions, should prove more than adequate when it comes to route finding. All of the walks were prepared using the Ordnance Survey 1:25,000 sheets that show the rights-of-way in our countryside. Despite the views of some critics, I would still recommend that you follow the perimeter of a field if your way is blocked by 6 foot high maize or wheat crops! The majority of paths used in these walks, however, are unlikely to be blocked by such obstructions.

For those who like to carry O.S. maps when out walking, the key 1:50,000 sheet is number 182 'Weston-super-Mare and Bridgwater'. Fourteen of the walks can be found on this sheet. Walk 1 around Harridge Wood is covered by sheet 183 'Yeovil and Frome' whilst part of walk 16 around Burrow Mump creeps on to sheet 193 'Taunton and Lyme Regis'. For the enthusiastic map readers, the appendices list the 1:25,000 Pathfinder sheets needed for each walk.

Refreshments

I have indicated where public-house, cafes and tea-rooms can be found on the walks. Most of the pubs en route allow children accompanied by adults on to their premises, usually into adjoining gardens. Teashop opening times vary according to the time of year and expected custom, but most can be relied upon to stay open until five or six o'clock during the summer months. Where no refreshment stops are found on the route itself, I have suggested picnic spots or convenient hostelries in the immediate area.

Conclusion

Do not forget the Country Code. Ramblers need the farmer as their friend, especially in an environmentally sensitive area like the Somerset Levels. It is a parent's duty to cultivate in their offspring a responsible attitude towards the countryside. Finally, I wish you as much pleasure in walking these routes as I had in preparing them. Good walking!

BALTONSBOROUGH CHURCH

Symbols used on the route maps

roads

settlement

river or stream

path or track

· 250′   selected spot heights

churches

hill-fort, bank or other antiquity

parking space

selected building for identification only

PH ·   public-house

direction indicator

deciduous woodland

A367
RADSTOCK   title and destination of selected road

number corresponding with directions

pond or lake

START   start of walk

coniferous woodland

THE DOULTING ROAD

Route 1   2½ miles
Nettlebridge and Harridge Wood

Outline   Nettlebridge ~ Harridge Wood ~ Stoke Bottom ~ Harridge Wood ~ Nettlebridge.

Summary   East of Wells, the Mendips lose some of their height and drama. However, there are still many delightful walks to be found, such as this circuit between Shepton Mallet and Radstock. Tucked away just off of the Foss Way at Nettlebridge lies Harridge Wood. Secretive valleys, tumbling streams, overhanging rock faces, caves and springs of freshwater have created a most tantalising natural landscape. Collinson described the area most beautifully in his 18th century 'History of Somerset':

"A country pleasingly divided with hills and valleys. Some of the valleys are deep, gloomy and picturesque, the acclivities clothed with hanging woods, intermixed with romantic rocks".

A short and relatively gentle circuit, that should lie within the capabilities of active toddlers as well as older children.

Attractions   Until the 20th century, Stoke Bottom was a thriving industrial hamlet. As many as 40 cottages, a mansion and a paper-mill were scattered about this now quite isolated valley. Today, all that remains of the settlement are a few decaying walls and the springtime snowdrops, remnants from the cottagers' cultivated gardens. What attracted the mill to this lonely spot were 'the quick streams and clear water', fed by the abundant flow from St. Dunstan's Well perched slightly up the hillside. The well is a splendid place, surrounded by small rocky outcrops that hide one or two small caves. This will prove a fascinating site for carefully supervised youngsters to explore. The well is fed by a small stream that disappears underground at Stoke Lane Slocker, some ¾ mile away. Incidentally, the ghost of the daughter of Stoke House is said to haunt these valleys! The victim of a broken love affair, she reputedly threw herself into the stream at Stoke Bottom and drowned!

Harridge Wood is a part of Mendip Forest, property of the Forestry Commission. In the Spring, the floor of the wood is quite literally covered in wild flowers, with bluebells, primroses, wood anemone and the odorous wild garlic being but the most common. An amusing diversion for youngsters is to see how many of the letters of the alphabet can be matched-up with a flower, a tree, a plant or a shrub within the woods.

continued on page 14

11

Route 1

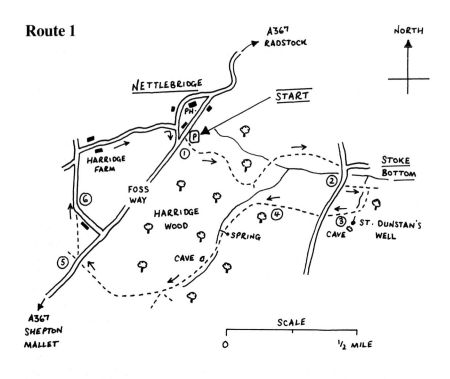

North

A367 RADSTOCK

NETTLEBRIDGE

START

PH.

P

HARRIDGE FARM

FOSS WAY

HARRIDGE WOOD

STOKE BOTTOM

St. DUNSTAN'S WELL

CAVE

SPRING

CAVE

A367 SHEPTON MALLET

SCALE

0   ½ MILE

DOG ROSE

12

Route 1

Nettlebridge and Harridge Wood   2½ miles

START   *Nettlebridge lies between Radstock and Shepton Mallet on the A367. As you approach the village from the north, bear left on to the minor road that runs parallel to the A367, a few yards beyond the Holcombe turning. In 200 yards, at the top of a rise, the entrance to Harridge Wood lies on the left-hand side. There is room for parking at the entrance to the wood. G.R. 648484.*

ROUTE

1. *The entrance to the wood is marked by a board signposted 'Mendip Forest-Harridge Wood'. Follow the main woodland path for close on ½ mile to a circular clearing in the trees. Fork left and follow the footpath downhill to a footbridge across a stream. Continue along the footpath beyond this bridge until you reach a stile, beyond which you emerge into an open field. Follow the fieldpath beyond the stile. It borders the stream on the right, before passing through a gateway to emerge at a road junction.*

2. *Turn right, along the road to Doulting. In 100 yards, just past a small transport depot, turn left on to an enclosed path. In 200 yards, the path crosses a stream that comes tumbling down from St. Dunstan's Well. Turn immediately to the right, to follow a footpath uphill to a gateway, beyond which lies St. Dunstan's Well.*

3. *At the gateway, turn right to follow the hedgerow on to the Nettlebridge to Doulting road. Cross the road, pass through the gateway opposite and bear sharply to the left. Follow the edge of the woodland across the field to a gateway, where the path passes into Harridge Wood.*

4. *Follow the main path through Harridge Wood for ½ mile, until you reach a junction of paths. Fork to the right and follow the path uphill alongside a boundary wall. At the top of the climb, look out for a stone slab stile in the wall ahead, ever so slightly to the right.*

5. *Beyond the stile, cross the field to the wall opposite, aiming for a stile that lies to the right of a bungalow. Cross the busy A367 beyond, and cross yet another stile slightly to the right. In the field beyond, aim for a gateway and stile in the far right-hand corner.*

6. *The path emerges on to a lane. Turn left, and in a short distance you will come to a staggered crossroads. Turn right - the left-turn is to Wells - and follow a cul-de-sac lane past a collection of farm buildings. In just under*

13

½ *mile, the lane dips down to join the A367.* **Cross the main road with extreme care,** *follow the pavement opposite to the right for just 100 yards, where a left-turn will return you to your vehicle.*

Public Transport A fairly regular bus service is operated by Badgerline Buses between Bath and Shepton Mallet, passing through Nettlebridge. There is no Sunday service.

———————

Anemone matches the letter 'A', bluebell the 'B' and so on. It should be possible to cover 15 letters of the alphabet with very little difficulty.

The final section of Harridge Wood, through a deep wooded valley with occasional rocky outcrops, is yet another watery paradise. The stream here ultimately flows into the Somerset Frome, and is fed hereabouts by any number of springs. Springs occur where a layer of porous material overlays a deeper impermeable bed of rock. Water can therefore only penetrate so far underground before bubbling out along a spring-line. It is not surprising that the water authorities have trapped the water sources in the valley, the rusting railings at various points encircling their sources of Adam's ale! With so many tempting spots for a paddle throughout this walk, don't forget to pack a towel into your rucksack.

Refreshments The Nettlebridge Inn, on the main A367 through the village, serves coffee and a range of bar snacks.

CHARTERHOUSE CHURCH

Route 2   3½ miles
Charterhouse and Velvet Bottom

Outline   Charterhouse ~ Long Wood ~ Black Rock ~ Velvet Bottom ~ Charterhouse.

Summary   This ramble explores some of the most interesting landscape to be found on Mendip, in and around the isolated hamlet of Charterhouse. The local lead deposits brought the Romans to the area, and it is likely that the Second Legion would have had barracks in this lonely outpost . . . no doubt directing the local slaves! In the valleys below Charterhouse lie three fascinating nature reserves -Long Wood, Black Rock and Velvet Bottom - whose very names conjure-up a vivid imagery. These reserves could not provide a greater contrast, with Long Wood being an area of broad-leaved woodland whilst Velvet Bottom is so saturated with lead deposits that there is scarcely a tree in sight. Whether your interest is in natural history, ancient history or industrial archaeology, you will find plenty to enthral you within the few brief miles of this circuit.

Attractions   The O.S. map shows both a 'Roman Fort' and a 'Roman Settlement' at Charterhouse. What brought the Romans to this remote Mendip outpost were the local lead deposits. The lead was widely used throughout the Roman Empire, one notable use being to line the Roman Baths at nearby Bath. A Roman Road ran across the Mendips to Old Sarum and the south coast ports, from where the riches of Charterhouse were shipped to all points of the Empire. The lead was worked as recently as the late 19th century by the Mendip Mining Company, when the chief activity was extracting lead from the plentiful Roman and Medieval refuse. Today, there are spoil tips, horizontal flues and washing pools, quietly reverting to a more natural landscape.

Adders, grass-snakes and slow-worms slide gently around the uneven gruffy ground, while sea campion surrounds the frog-infested pools. Of the Romans, there is little other than an occasional mound and the isolated pottery fragment or coin churned-up by the plough.

Long Wood, Black Rock and Velvet Bottom are all nature reserves controlled by the Somerset Trust for Nature Conservation. Long Wood is 42 acres of old, mainly broadleaved woodland, Black Rock is 183 acres of rough grassland, woodland and scree, whilst Velvet Bottom is a dry river valley that has been the scene of extensive lead workings over many centuries. The natural history of these reserves is so rich and varied that

continued on page 18

B   15

Route 2

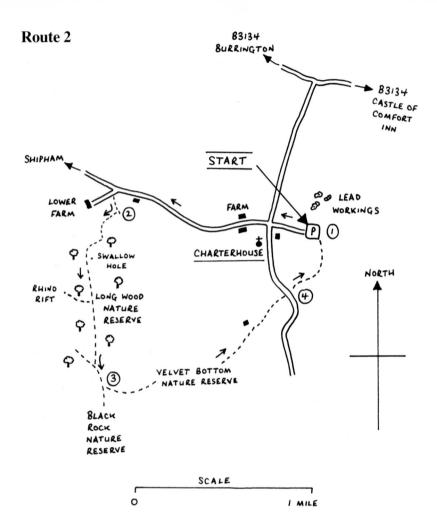

B3134
BURRINGTON

B3134
CASTLE OF
COMFORT
INN

START

SHIPHAM

LOWER
FARM

②

FARM

LEAD
WORKINGS

P ①

SWALLOW
HOLE

CHARTERHOUSE

RHINO
RIFT

LONG WOOD
NATURE
RESERVE

④

NORTH

③

VELVET BOTTOM
NATURE RESERVE

BLACK
ROCK
NATURE
RESERVE

SCALE

0   1 MILE

16

Route 2

Charterhouse and Velvet Bottom

3½ miles

START *Charterhouse lies 1 mile south of the B3134 road, midway between Burrington Combe and the Castle of Comfort Inn. As you enter this small hamlet, turn left at the cross-roads into the parking area at the Blackmoor Lead Workings. G.R. 505557.*

ROUTE

1. *Return to the cross-roads and follow the lane opposite signposted to Shipham. In ¾ mile, bear left at a distinct fork, 100 yards beyond an isolated bungalow. In a matter of yards, turn left on to a track.*

2. *50 yards along this track, at the bottom of a dip, cross the stile in the hedgerow on the right-hand side. In the field beyond, bear right until you come to a stile and some steps that lead down into Long Wood Nature Reserve. An obvious path heads southwards for ¾ mile through this area of broadleaved woodland.*

3. *At the end of Long Wood, turn left at a junction. In a short distance, you will emerge into Black Rock Nature Reserve. Almost immediately, cross the stone slab stile on the left into Velvet Bottom Nature Reserve. An obvious path through Velvet Bottom brings you eventually to the Charterhouse to Cheddar road.*

7. *Cross the road, and follow the path opposite through the gruffy ground of the Blackmoor Lead Workings. It is but a few yards back to the parking area.*

Public Transport None available.

ALDER

the interested observer is advised to purchase the selection of leaflets available at Black Rock Gate on the B3135 at the head of Cheddar Gorge. A particular highlight of Long Wood is a profusion of pot-holes and caves. At the entrance to the reserve, Long Wood Swallet devours the waters of a local stream that emerges into the daylight again some 24 hours later at the foot of Cheddar Gorge. Half-way down the reserve, a small path on the right leads to Rhino Rift Cave, so called because a tooth of the woolly rhinoceros was found near the entrance, together with teeth of hyena! Back on the main path, you will pass the site of Longwood Valley Sink. This sink hole appeared in 1968, when a blow-hole appeared at the spot following a notorious flood. The hole is still being excavated, with 900 truck-loads of waste - weighing a massive 30 tons - having been removed from below ground by the start of 1990.

The smooth, soft grasses that bedeck Velvet Bottom make its name wholly appropriate. The dry grassland hereabouts is renowned for its large population of lizards and adders. Adders can grow to a length of 2 feet, and are recognisable by their triangular heads and zig-zag markings. Their diet consists of lizards and small mammals such as mice, as well as frogs. The vipera berus enjoys nothing more than basking in dry sunny places and, if left undisturbed, is most unlikely to inflict you with its venomous bite!

Refreshments Charterhouse is 'dry' as is the rest of this ramble. The site of the Blackmoor Lead Workings at the end of the walk provides many fine picnicking spots, an altogether healthier alternative!

PRIDDY POND

18

Route 3   4 miles
Priddy Mineries and North Hill

Outline   Stock Hill Plantation ~ Priddy Mineries ~ Eastwater Farm ~ North Hill ~ Priddy Mineries ~ Stock Hill Plantation.

Summary   Rock folding has pushed the underlying impervious sandstone to the surface at just 4 points on Mendip - Blackdown, North Hill, Pen Hill and Beacon Hill. These are the high points on the hills. This ramble explores the area around North Hill, whose summit just registers the 1,000 foot mark. Round barrows, a fine pot-hole and disused lead workings all add to the interest. This is a really exhilarating 4 miles ... but do pick fine and dry weather. The hilltops of Mendips are bleak places indeed during a force 10 gale, and the local drove tracks can resemble disused canals following periods of heavy rainfall!

Attractions   Priddy Mineries is today a nature reserve of some repute. Until 1908, however, the St. Cuthbert's Leadworks worked the land for the soft grey metal that would literally drive the miners mad. The rough bumpy ground is known locally as 'gruffy' ground on account of its 'groovy' nature. The archaeological remains include several flues, the ruinous mine buildings, prominent slag heaps and one or two pools where the ore was washed. Leaded gruffy ground supports little vegetation other than grass scrub, although it is a paradise for lizards, slow worms, grass snakes and adders. The pools are said to contain large numbers of crested newts, whilst the damp microclimate is a haven for several species of dragonfly.

Eastwater Cavern is one of the many pot-holes that riddle the Mendip landscape. The cracks and joints that divide the limestone have, over the years, been widened and expanded by the action of slightly acidic rainwater to form a caver's paradise. Eastwater was unblocked of its mud and debris in the Spring of 1902 by Herbert Balch, a great pioneer of Mendip caving, together with a band of 20 local labourers hired at £5 a day! The farmer at nearby Manor Farm had refused access to Swildon's Hole, which lay on his land, and Balch anticipated that Eastwater would provide an alternative gateway to the local subterranean world. Gradually, passages with such descriptive names as the Mud Escalator and the Boulder Ruckle were opened up. The fatality that occurred in Eastwater on 31st July 1960, when a young caver was hit by a rock fall at the bottom of Boulder Ruckle, should serve as a warning to any youngster as to the dangers of pot-holing. Never venture underground unless accompanied by experienced cavers!   *continued on page 22*

Route 3

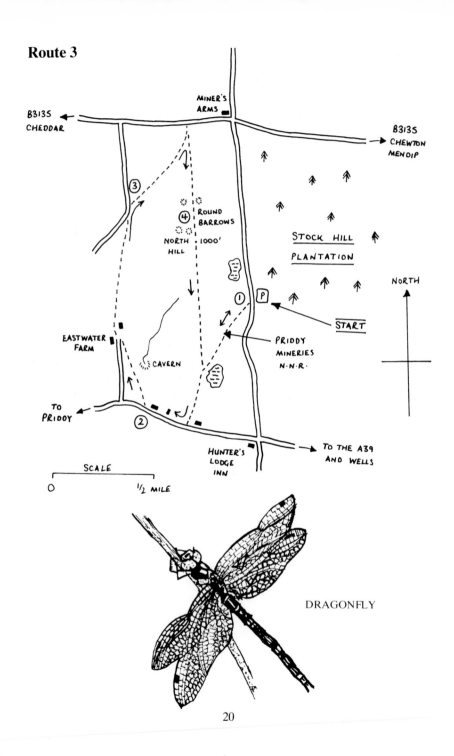

B3135
CHEDDAR

MINER'S ARMS

B3135
CHEWTON MENDIP

③

④ ROUND BARROWS

NORTH HILL · 1000'

STOCK HILL PLANTATION

NORTH

① P

START

EASTWATER FARM

CAVERN

PRIDDY MINERIES N·N·R·

TO PRIDDY

②

HUNTER'S LODGE INN

TO THE A39 AND WELLS

SCALE

0   ½ MILE

DRAGONFLY

Route 3
Priddy Mineries and North Hill   4 miles

START   *Turn left at the Miner's Arms Hotel, which lies midway between Chewton Mendip and Priddy on the B3135. In ¾ mile, on the left-hand side, park in the Forestry Commission's Stock Hill car-park. G.R. 548513.*

ROUTE

1. *Cross the road, and follow the path opposite as it bears to the left across the Priddy Mineries Nature Reserve. Continue along the path as it passes a large pond, before emerging on to the Priddy road. Turn right and follow the road for 200 yards past several houses to reach a gateway on the right-hand side.*

2. *Enter the field beyond this gateway and cross diagonally to the left to reach the clearly visible Eastwater Farm. The path passes to the left of Eastwater Cavern, which lies in the dip in the field. Beyond the farm, continue along Eastwater Drove until a quiet country lane is reached.*

3. *Enter the field on the right by means of a handgate. The barrows on the hilltop ahead are the next target, but the right-of-way is somewhat circuitous! Head uphill bearing to the left to a gate in the far left-hand corner of the field, then almost immediately double-back on yourself to reach the barrows.*

4. *Aim for a second group of barrows on the hilltop ahead, and a handgate in the corner of the field. Follow the wall beyond the handgate back downhill to reach the large pond passed earlier on the walk. You will cross one stile en route, whilst keeping the field boundary on your right-hand side. At the pond, turn left to retrace your steps to the Stock Hill car-park.*

Public Transport   The higher parts of Mendip are virtually lacking in any form of public transport unless you care to hire a taxi!

Two groups of tumuli - Ashen Hill Barrows and Priddy Nine Barrows - dominate North Hill. The barrows date from the Bronze Age, when it was usual for the local chieftain to be laid to rest on the high ground above his settlement. It probably had not a little to do with being nearer his gods! Excavations at the site have revealed Bronze Age weapons, various domestic implements and funerary ceramics. These relics can be viewed at the Bristol City Museum. The barrow groups make a fine skyline site, making these Mendip heights in the autumnal mists a particularly eerie spot. Indeed, locals walking along the adjoining Nine Barrows Lane are fond of commenting that 'it's almost as though people do be peering over the hedge at you'. You have been warned!

Refreshments Just minutes from the start of the walk are two of the best-known hostelries on Mendip - the Miner's Arms and Hunter's Lodge Inn (see the map). For many years, the Miner's Arms restaurant has been renowned for its 'Priddy Snail Butter' . . . which is one ingenious solution to the local snail problem!

CHEDDAR GORGE

22

Cheddar and the Gorge

Outline   Cheddar ~ Piney Sleight Farm ~ Black Rock Nature Reserve ~ Jacob's Ladder ~ Cheddar.

Summary   Cheddar Gorge, with its towering cliffs and craggy rock formations, represents one of the most spectacular natural features within the British Isles. There is really but one way to explore the wonders of this corner of Mendip, and that is to follow the footpaths that climb high above the gorge itself. Not only do these paths bring fine vantage points across the landscape, they also enable the walker to obtain some degree of seclusion by escaping the crowds and the traffic in the gorge below. The outward leg of this circuit climbs over 650 feet from Cheddar village on to the Mendip hilltops above Piney Sleight Farm, with a compensatory descent following on the return into Cheddar. Perhaps a rather strenuous family walk, best suited for the older and more active youngster!

Attractions   'The incline became steeper, the winding more intense. The boulders suddenly became high, vertical precipices of limestone, with tall trees growing out of them. Then it became even grander, and more awe-inspiring. In the high gale I felt certain that the rocks were going to fall on me. The cliffs assumed shapes - a lion here, a monkey there'. It is over 50 years since S.P.B. Mais penned this vivid description of Cheddar Gorge, and the passage of time has done little to diminish what must surely rank as some of our finest inland cliff scenery.

The gorge was carved out by running water in centuries long past. Rainwater contains a mild solution of acid, which readily dissolves the cracks and joints found in the Mendip limestone. The same process explains the many caves and caverns that honeycomb the local subterranean landscape. The running water is still there, but only the pot-holers can testify to its existence. The cliffs rise to over 500 feet in height, and are dotted with squat yew trees and whitebeam, rare alpine pennygrass and the unique Cheddar pink. The rock ledges provide nesting grounds for the many jackdaws whose squawks echo incessantly around the gorge.

At the foot of the cliffs in Cheddar are a collection of show caves, the most noted of which are Cox's and Gough's. George Cox discovered his collection of underground passages in the 1830s, and contained within are spectacular stalagmite pillars and stalactite curtains, together with

continued on page 26

Route 4

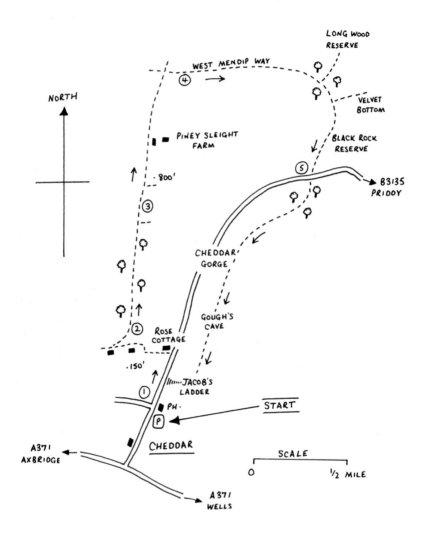

Route 4

Cheddar and the Gorge $\qquad$ 5 miles

START   *Cheddar lies just off the A371 Wells to Axbridge road. A short distance north of the A371, on the 'B' class road that leads up into the gorge, you will find the Butcher's Arms P.H. on the right-hand side. Alongside the public-house is a local authority car-park. G.R. 461537.*

ROUTE

1. *Leave the car-park, turn right and follow the road up through the lower part of Cheddar Gorge for just over ⅓ mile. Just beyond a small Water Board reservoir, on the left-hand side, you will come to Rose Cottage. Turn left immediately in front of this cottage, and follow the unmetalled track ahead. Shortly, in front of a driveway leading to a house, the path bears right to pass behind a cottage. The path brings you out behind another dwelling. Here, follow the path that slopes back up the hill to the right.*

2. *Follow the obvious path uphill for almost ½ mile, as it follows the wooded western slopes of the gorge. The woodland eventually thins out, and the path crosses a stile on the left-hand side. Beyond this stile, the path bears right to follow the right-hand field boundary - an overgrown, tumbledown wall - on up the hillside for nearly ½ mile. Ignore all right turns, continuing on uphill until just beyond an area of scrubland you reach the open Mendip plateau. A flagstone stile, at over 800 feet, roughly marks the spot from where excellent views across the Somerset Levels to Glastonbury and beyond can be enjoyed.*

3. *Beyond the stile, the path follows the left-hand field boundary across three fields to Piney Sleight Farm. Pass to the left of the farmhouse, and follow the enclosed farm drive for some 300 yards until a stile and a signpost on the right-hand side point you in the direction of Cheddar via the West Mendip Way.*

4. *Follow the right-hand field boundary for ½ mile until a stile takes you into Long Wood. After passing through a fine avenue of hazel trees, the path emerges into Black Rock Reserve. Follow the main path through this dry limestone valley for ½ mile until you reach the B3135 Cheddar road.*

5. *Cross the B3135, climb the stile opposite and a short but steep ascent through the trees will bring you to the high ground at the top end of Cheddar Gorge. Follow the well-worn path towards Cheddar, ignoring one prominent left-turn to Draycott. The path back to Cheddar passes high above the cliffs on the eastern side of the gorge, where there are*

unfenced sheer drops of several hundred feet! Eventually, the path brings you to the top of Jacob's Ladder. Descend the 300 steps to reach the road, turn left and within minutes you will back at the car-park.

Public Transport   Badgerline operate a regular bus service between Weston-super-Mare and Wells, that passes through Cheddar.

---

strange rock formations with equally strange names such as 'Mermaid and Mummy' and 'Lady Chapel'. Gough's was discovered in the 1890s, although the bones and primitive tools contained within dated back to palaeolithic man. The 12,000 year old skeleton of what has been referred to as 'Cheddar man' was found in Gough's in 1903, and is exhibited today in the cave's museum.

The Black Rock Nature Reserve at the head of Cheddar Gorge consists of 183 acres of rough grassland, plantation, natural woodland and scree, all sited in and around a dry limestone valley. Within the reserve lies the former Black Rock Quarry, with clearly exposed sections of limestone. It is easy to spot the vertical cracks or 'joints' in the rock through which the rainwater drains away very quickly. This results in a dry valley, with the rivers and streams deep underground flowing through elaborate cave and tunnel systems. Alongside the former workings is an old lime-kiln. Lime was produced by heating the limestone rock from the quarry with coal or charcoal. The lime was then used either in mortar for strengthening walls, or it was spread on the fields of the Mendip plateau where leaching by heavy rainfall removes the natural lime from the soil.

Refreshments   In Cheddar village, there are any number of refreshment facilities including tea-shops and chip-shops. At the end of the walk, there is also the Butcher's Arms P.H.

Compton Bishop and Crook Peak

Outline   Compton Bishop ~ Compton House ~ Crook Peak ~
Compton Bishop.

Summary   The Mendip uplands tend to be characterised by high
plateaux rather than genuine peaks. Above the isolated village of
Compton Bishop, however, Crook Peak is one notable exception. Here
we have a genuine summit, a pinnacle that gives the false impression of
being the highest point on these hills. To youngsters, it does not take
much imagination to think of Crook Peak as a mountain in miniature,
whose rocky summit is the ultimate target of this short ramble. To
seasoned veterans, however, its mere 628 feet will register as little more
than a pimple! An excellent little walk, arguably the best on Mendip.

Attractions   The hilltops above Compton Bishop, that embrace both
Crook Peak and Wavering Down, were acquired by the National Trust in
March 1986. The whole area is a 'Site of Special Scientific Interest' on
account of its rich variety of grassland and woodland habitats, 719 acres of
what is effectively common land that lies within the Mendip Hills 'Area of
Outstanding Natural Beauty'. Such designations are testimony indeed to
the quality of the natural environment hereabouts, which has been
described as 'a walker's delight with its short dry turf, wide views and
wildlife'. This is undoubtedly some of the best scenery to be found on
Mendip.

Overlooking this corner of the hills is Crook Peak, which to
travellers on the nearby M5 motorway would appear to be the highest
point on the hills. It actually falls 400 feet below the triangulation pillar on
Blackdown, high above Burrington Combe, which at 1,067 feet is the true
high-point on Mendip. The name 'Crook' is due to the rocky outcrop at
the summit, which is said to resemble a 'crook' or packhorse saddle. Such
high landmarks inevitably became sites for beacons in centuries past.
Confirmation of this fact can be found in the nearby village of Banwell,
where the churchwarden's accounts for 1580 make interesting reading. A
reference to the sum of 5 shillings 'pd the firste day of July for one load of
wood for the Beaken and for carryinge of the same to Croke Peke' can be
found. Some old Admiralty charts actually mark the Peak as 'see me not',
an indication of its unreliability as a landmark. This can be put down to
the fact that low cloud often envelops the summit.

continued on page 30

Route 5

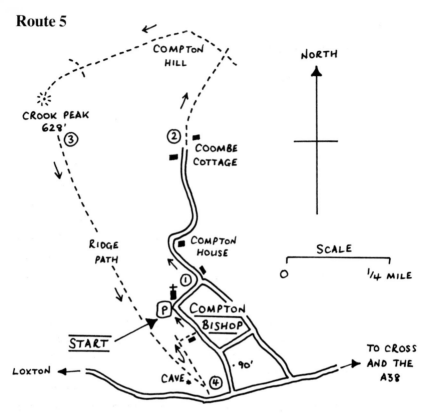

NORTH

SCALE

0   1/4 MILE

COMPTON HILL

CROOK PEAK 628'

③

② COOMBE COTTAGE

RIDGE PATH

COMPTON HOUSE

①

P

✝

START

COMPTON BISHOP

LOXTON

CAVE ✱

④

· 90'

TO CROSS AND THE A38

THE MENDIPS FROM CROOK PEAK

Route 5

Compton Bishop and Crook Peak   3 miles

START   *The village of Compton Bishop lies 2 miles west of the A38 at Cross near Axbridge. Follow the signs to the village and park in the vicinity of the village church. G.R. 396554.*

ROUTE

1. *Follow Church Lane down in front of St. Andrew's Church for just 100 yards where you turn left into Coombe Lane. Follow this quiet cul-de-sac uphill for almost ½ mile until you reach Coombe Cottage. En route, you will pass through a gateway where a sign declares this to be a 'Private Lane'. This prohibition only relates to motor vehicles.*

2. *Beyond Coombe Cottage, the lane becomes a stony footpath that is followed uphill to the hilltop. Turn left at the hilltop fence, and head westwards to the obvious summit of Crook Peak, some ¾ mile distant. Ignore any side turns that might tempt you.*

3. *As you climb towards the summit of Crook Peak, notice the ridge that bears away to the left. From the rocky hilltop, follow this ridge for the return leg to Compton Bishop. In a little over ½ mile, you will pass one or two rocky openings in the ground that the O.S. map has the audacity to describe as 'caves'. In a short distance, just before reaching the Cross road, the ridge path you have been following will join a cross track.*

4. *Turn left at this junction, and follow a shady path for several hundred yards until you come to a gateway on your right. Follow the path beyond this gate to a road junction, alongside Manor Farm. Turn left, and it is but a few yards back to St. Andrew's Church.*

Public Transport   Compton Bishop is not served by public transport.

Cloud permitting, the view from the summit is particularly fine. Looking south, and reading from left to right, the landmarks include Wavering Down, Cheddar Reservoir, Glastonbury Tor, Brent Knoll and the M5, Hinkley Point and Bridgwater Bay, the Bristol Channel and Brean Down. Whilst adults check-out such incidentals, youngsters will undoubtedly enjoy scrambling over the limestone outcrops at the summit.

Compton Bishop is a picturesque village nestled at the foot of a fold in the Mendip Hills. The centre of village life is the Parish Church of St. Andrew, consecrated by Bishop Jocelin on 13th July 1236. Old ecclesiastical buildings become fascinating places to explore if you invest a few pence in the church guidebook. At Compton Bishop, for example, I discovered that the magnificent 14th century carved stone pulpit is one of the best known specimens of its ilk in the whole of Somerset, whilst the ancient oak chest in the nave once acted as a depository for parish offerings to the poor. Perhaps the highlight of the church is the 14th century churchyard cross ... whose history is best discovered by purchasing the church guide!

Refreshments   There are no refreshments on this walk. However, back on the A38 at Cross, both the White Hart and the New Inn serve meals and snacks.

WILD STRAWBERRY

30

Route 6   4 miles
Wookey Hole and Ebbor Gorge

Outline   Wookey Hole ~ Ebbor Gorge ~ Higher Pitts Farm ~ Lower Milton ~ Wookey Hole.

Summary   Wookey Hole village, with its fine showcaves, is one of the great attractions of Mendip. Any feelings of claustrophobia, however, will soon disappear as you climb over 700 feet on to the bare and open hilltops that tower above the village. What makes this climb particularly exciting is the rocky scramble that the path takes up through Ebbor Gorge. This dry Mendip valley, whose caves once sheltered wolves, bears and ancient man, is not for the faint-hearted! The views from the hilltops reach deep into the Somerset Levels, although the eye will inevitably focus upon Glastonbury Tor, the very heart of Avalon.

Attractions   The caves at Wookey have been carved out of the Mendip limestone by the subterranean River Axe. As visitors are shown around deep underground, seemingly innocuous limestone formations are transformed into creatures of legend by highly imaginative tour guides. One pair of stalagmites are allegedly the petrified remains of a witch and her dog, turned to stone when a monk doused them with holy water! Visitors were flocking to the caves as far back as 1709, when a party of six were charged 2/6 (12½p) to see the caves. The admission charge included candles and beer, but not the elaborate catwalks and atmospheric lighting that today's visitor enjoys. The Wookey complex also includes a traditional paper mill, a fine collection of fairground memorabilia and a small waxworks. To complete the holiday atmosphere, there is a Victorian penny arcade that will inevitably invoke feelings of nostalgia amongst the more mature visitor!

Ebbor Gorge is a National Nature Reserve, managed by the Nature Conservancy Council and leased from the National Trust. The gorge is typical of limestone country - it was carved out by an ancient river that has long since disappeared beneath the permeable limestone. Within the gorge, joints and fissures have been enlarged by the passage of rain-water, leaving behind small caves and rock shelters where the remains of reindeer, bears, wolves and lemmings have been found by archaeologists. Neolithic man also sought shelter in these caves around 3,000 B.C., and his various remains - bones, tools, and ornaments - can be seen in the museum at the Wookey Hole complex.

continued on page 34

Route 6

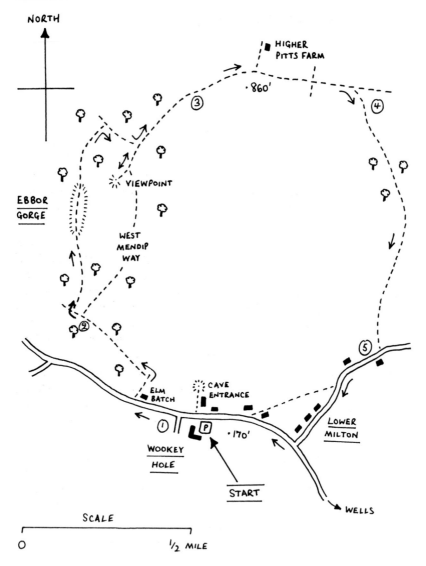

NORTH

HIGHER
PITTS FARM

·860'

③

④

EBBOR
GORGE

VIEWPOINT

WEST
MENDIP
WAY

②

⑤

ELM
BATCH

CAVE
ENTRANCE

LOWER
MILTON

①

P

·170'

WOOKEY
HOLE

START

WELLS

SCALE

0   ½ MILE

32

Route 6

Wookey Hole and Ebbor Gorge   4 miles

START *Wookey Hole, with its caves and museum complex, lies just 2 miles north-west of Wells. This major tourist attraction is clearly signposted from what is England's smallest city. There is a large car-park at the caves site. G.R. 532476.*

ROUTE

1. *Leave Wookey Hole car-park and turn left to follow the road through the village. Alongside Elm Batch, a bungalow on the edge of the village, turn right through a gateway where a marker-post indicates Priddy 3 miles. In a matter of yards, follow the path that forks to the left to pass through a delightful wooded valley. In ¼ mile, you will reach a stile at the entrance to the Ebbor Gorge Nature Reserve.*

2. *Continue along the path through the reserve until, in a few hundred yards, you take the second of two adjoining turnings on the right-hand side, signposted to 'The Gorge'. After a steep, rocky climb of several hundred feet, the path reaches a junction at the hilltop where you turn right. Shortly, another junction is reached where you turn left to continue the climb out of Ebbor Nature Reserve. N.B. It is worth turning right at this second junction to reach a viewpoint overlooking the gorge, before retracing your steps - see the map.*

3. *The path climbs to the hilltop where you continue along the edge of the hill in the general direction of the distant Pen Hill T.V. mast, always keeping the stone wall to your left. After two or three hilltop fields, you will reach a gateway where the path emerges into an open field. A yellow arrow on the gate points diagonally to the right.*

4. *Head half-right across this field to the hedgerow at the far side. Pass through the gateway in this hedge and follow the track beyond down through a patch of woodland and across some fields to the road at Lower Milton.*

5. *Turn right, and follow the road back to Wookey Hole as shown on the map. (The footpath shown on the map is difficult to follow).*

Public Transport Badgerline operate buses from Wells to Wookey Hole.

33

The gorge is surrounded by deciduous woodland, which is both carefully managed and conserved by the Nature Conservancy Council. The woodland at the foot of the gorge contains ash, elm, beech and oak, together with herbaceous plants such as dog's mercury, enchanter's nightshade and hart's tongue fern. Badgers are plentiful here, and you may notice their tracks left when in search of berries and beetles. On the rather more rocky slopes of the gorge itself, vegetation characteristic of such an upland environment is found - dogwood, spindle, whitebeam and buckthorn. The excellent display centre next to the Ebbor Gorge car-park (which lies slightly off of the course of this walk) gives a full account of the natural history and geology of the area.

The view from the top of the cliffs above the gorge is truly spectacular. Here the path is some 800 feet above sea-level, and spread out panoramically beneath are the Somerset Levels, Wookey and Wells to the east, and the Tor at Glastonbury standing out as a prominent land-mark. In the background, far away to the south and west, lie the Quantock Hills and Exmoor.

Refreshments There are plenty of refreshment facilities in and around the caves complex at Wookey, although a more pleasant alternative would be a picnic to be enjoyed at the viewpoint above Ebbor Gorge.

NORTH WOTTON CHURCH

Around North Wootton

Outline   North Wootton ~ North Wootton Vineyard ~ Stoodly Hill ~ Folly Wood ~ North Wootton.

Summary   An interesting circuit that explores the eastern fringe of the Mendip Hills around the village of North Wootton. A ford, a fascinating vineyard, secluded woodland and enticing glimpses of Glastonbury Tor all add to the interest along the route. Stoodly Hill presents something of a climb, but the fine views that open-up offer more than adequate compensation. A rewarding excursion into a little explored corner of Somerset, that offers a complete contrast to the tourist honeypots further west at Cheddar, Wookey and Wells. The guide-book that described North Wootton as 'being off the beaten track' was spot-on!

Attractions   North Wootton, and the neighbouring village of Pilton, have developed quite a name in recent years as a wine-producing centre of some repute. The area is on the eastern fringe of the Mendip Hills, and the south facing slopes provide ideal conditions for viticulture. Wine production is no new thing in Somerset, however. Back in the 14th century, the Abbot of Glastonbury had extensive vineyards that supplied his table with the choicest of wines! A slight detour from the main walk - see the map - will bring you to the North Wootton Vineyard. The vines and business premises are open to the public from Monday to Saturday.

Cider is obviously the beverage for which Somerset is most well known. Years ago, there was a traditional cider press at North Wootton's Crossways Inn. Alternate layers of apples and straw were placed into the press before being squeezed to extract the juices. The nearby Rural Life Museum at Glastonbury has occasional displays of the historic art of cider making, whilst it is possible to purchase the local scrumpy at the village store in Pilton. Apple orchards are widespread within the county, indeed you will pass a small orchard on the lane between North Wootton and Nut Tree Farm.

The tracks, woodland paths and bridleways followed on this walk are festooned with wild flowers during the Spring and Summer months. In the shady glades beside the Redlake at Stoodly Bridge, wood anemones, primroses and wild garlic flourish during the early springtime, whilst Folly Wood offers an attractive display of bluebells. Other flora and fauna to keep your eyes open for on the route include the noisy rookery some distance north of Stoodly Hill, and the small pond alongside Folly

continued on page 38

Route 7

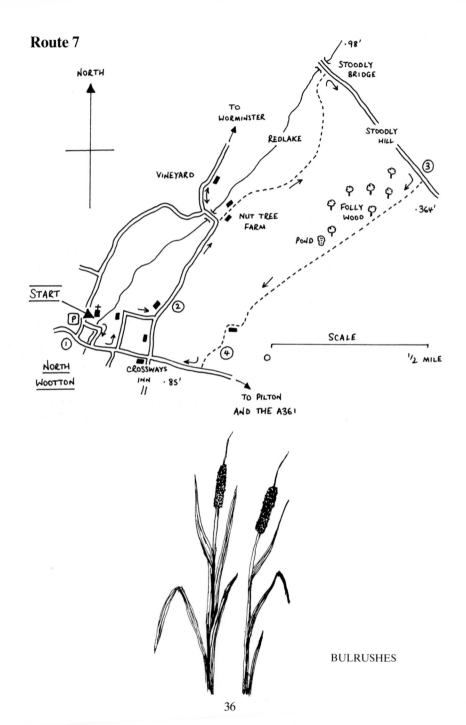

NORTH

·98'
STOODLY
BRIDGE

TO
WORMINSTER

REDLAKE

STOODLY
HILL

③

VINEYARD

·364'

NUT TREE
FARM

FOLLY
WOOD

POND

START

②

①

NORTH
WOOTTON

CROSSWAYS
INN ·85'

④

SCALE

O   ½ MILE

TO PILTON
AND THE A361

BULRUSHES

36

Route 7

Around North Wootton   3 miles

START   *Leave the A361 Glastonbury to Shepton Mallet road at Pilton, 6 miles east of Glastonbury. Follow the signs to North Wootton, and park alongside the church at the western end of the village. G.R. 564418.*

ROUTE

1. *Follow the lane past the church, cross the Redlake and turn right to reach the 'main' road through the village. Continue to follow the road pattern as shown on the map.*

2. *Head northwards along the Worminster road for just under ½ mile to Nut Tree Farm. The road bears left at this point to continue to North Wootton Vineyard - an interesting diversion. The main walk continues straight ahead, past Nut Tree Farm, along an often muddy track to eventually reach Stoodly Bridge. Turn right at the road, and climb steeply up Stoodly Hill.*

3. *At the hilltop, bear right to follow the bridlepath that borders Folly Wood. Keep to the main path alongside the woodland, avoiding any tempting left or right turns. The path leaves the woodland by means of a handgate alongside a small pond. Beyond this handgate, follow the hedgerows directly ahead through the first two fields. In the third field, bear half left to reach a stile in the trees opposite.*

4. *Beyond the stile, follow a lane downhill to reach the North Wootton road. Turn right, and it is but a short distance back to the centre of the village and the church. On the way, you will pass the Crossways Inn.*

Public Transport   North Wootton is not served by a regular bus service.

Wood with its plentiful stock of bulrushes and water-boatmen. The Usborne Spotters Guide entitled 'Country Walks' should be a must for any youngster on this walk, with fresh discoveries turning up around every bend!

Throughout the walk, there are some fine open views of this corner of Somerset. Between Nut Tree Farm and Stoodly Bridge, the view to the north extends across Dulcote Hill and away to the more distant Pen Hill above Wells, with its vast I.B.A. transmitter. Returning to North Wootton from Folly Wood, the view away to the south-west is dominated by Glastonbury Tor, with the prominent tower of the ruinous St. Michael's Church. The exposed rock faces away on Dulcote Hill serve as a reminder that quarrying is big business in East Mendip. At nearby Merehead, on the Shepton Mallet to Frome road, lies the largest quarry in Western Europe, complete with its own railhead. The limestone of Mendip is used extensively as an aggregate in road building, and its extraction is a vital part of the local economy. The environmental impact of quarrying, however, has caused much alarm in Somerset, with the problem it generates being vividly described in Shirley Toulson's book 'The Mendip Hills: A Threatened Landscape' (Gollancz).

Refreshments   At the end of the walk in North Wootton, sustenance can be obtained at the Crossways Inn. One guidebook notes that the Crossways 'has a good reputation for pub food which has spread far and wide'.

RURAL LIFE MUSEUM, GLASTONBURY (Route 10)

Route 8   2½ miles

Around Brent Knoll

Outline   East Brent ~ Manor Farm ~ Brent Knoll ~ East Brent.

Summary   Brent Knoll is, quite unknowingly, the best known landmark in the whole of Somerset. Millions of motorists struggling down the M5 motorway to the West Country each summer must gaze on her slopes from the nearby service station and long for those open spaces and seclusion. The Knoll, a strange islanded hill, dominates the western edges of Somerset's central plain. Akin to Glastonbury Tor some miles to the east, Brent Knoll towers over the surrounding Levels, a lonely outpost of the underlying rock formation. As with many other knolls and tors, there is the inevitable legend. This is allegedly a shovelful of earth thrown down by the Devil when he was digging out the nearby Cheddar Gorge! Another feature that is shared with Glastonbury Tor is the general description of the circuit . . . what the walk lacks in miles is made up for by the steep ascent of the Knoll itself. This is a scant price to pay, however, for the panorama to be had from the hilltop. To quote S.P.B. Mais 'the view on every side is tremendous, being completely uninterrupted'.

Attractions   Old churches provide a wealth of intrigue and fascination for those prepared to invest a few minutes in their investigation. St. Mary's at East Brent, with its magnificent slender spire, is no exception. The church guidebook lists a staggering 38 features of interest for the visitor to discover! The fine nave ceiling of 1637 is certainly one highlight. It has been likened to a fretwork or cake-icing. The intricate plasterwork was the work of an Italian craftsman, who used the blackberry thorn as the main motif. The carved bench-ends are another pleasing feature of the church, those in the nave with poppy heads having been brought to East Brent from Glastonbury by Abbot John Selwood in the 15th century. My particular favourite piece is the memorial window in the chancel, dedicated to Prebendary Archdale Palmer Wickham, vicar of the parish from 1911-35. The Prebendary was both a keen naturalist and cricketer, themes that the stained glass vividly illustrates. Incidentally, I wonder if you can guess why the decorations on the central part of the West Gallery differ from those on each side? To find out, you really will have to make a donation to church funds and purchase the guidebook!

In the shadow of Brent Knoll lies Manor Farm, where the footpath passes a fine group of traditional stone farm buildings. This is the place where youngsters equipped with an 'I-spy on the farm' book will soon be

continued on page 42

39

Route 8

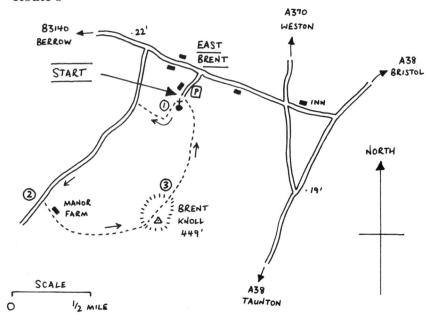

SCALE

0 ————— 1/2 MILE

BRENT KNOLL FROM CROOK PEAK

Route 8

Around Brent Knoll   2½ miles

START   *East Brent lies just west of the A38, 4 miles north of Highbridge. Park carefully in Church Road, the cul-de-sac lane that leads to St. Mary's Church. G.R. 344519.*

ROUTE

1. *Follow the path to the right of the church, ignoring the signposted left turn to Brent Knoll. At the top of the churchyard, the path goes to the right and passes through a kissing gate. Beyond this gate, continue straight ahead across the field to join Hill Lane. Turn left, and follow Hill Lane for ½ mile until you reach Manor Farm.*

2. *Turn left, pass the farm buildings and then follow the most direct and obvious route to the top of Brent Knoll. The right-of-way is well used and detailed description is unnecessary. The key details are to aim for the opposite gateway in the first field beyond the farm, beyond which the right-hand hedgerow is followed to the hilltop. Having explored the fortifications and taken in the expansive views, aim for the flag-pole at the northern end of the Knoll.*

3. *The path descends the steep hillside beneath the flag-pole for 100 yards before reaching a stile. Beyond the stile, keep walking in the direction of East Brent Church. The field paths are well-used, and a steady succession of waymarked stiles indicate the route. The path eventually passes through the school playground in East Brent before reaching the church.*

Public Transport   Badgerline Buses operate an express service between Bristol and Taunton which passes the Knoll Inn at East Brent.

notching up several hundred points. It may be a herd of steaming cattle in the byre, it could be the occasional free-range chicken, maybe the farmer out with his muck spreader, or even a sighting of the trusty old sheep dog. At least the slopes surrounding Brent Knoll have escaped the plough, and provide welcome relief from the tide of cereal crops that seem to be engulfing so much of Britain! The small fields and hedgerows hereabouts should be treasured and savoured.

Brent Knoll almost literally rises like an island from the surrounding Levels of Central Somerset. The triangulation pillar stands at the 450 feet mark, and commemorates various Jubilees and Coronations. Most recently, this was the site of the Jubilee bonfire in 1977. The hilltop was fortified by Iron Age settlers, and their defensive ramparts are remarkably well-preserved. Youngsters can enjoy re-enacting a past invasion! The remains of the Iron Age pottery fragments found on the site can be seen at the Woodspring Museum in nearby Weston. This tradition of defence continued right up to the last war, when trenches were excavated on the hilltop for use by the Home Guard. The views from Brent Knoll were rightly described by Mais as 'tremendous'. The only surprise is that a topograph has not been placed on the site. I will leave you to sort out the details, suffice to say that Glastonbury Tor, the Quantocks, Exmoor, Bridgwater Bay, the Bristol Channel and the Mendips are all within sight of the hilltop.

The third Thursday in August is the busiest day in the East Brent calendar - Harvest Home. The festivities last all day, a giant marquee is erected and the locals process through the village led by a band to eventually partake of a veritable feast. The length of the marquee is lined with ivy ropes, whilst hoops and banners, corn and flowers add to the colour of the scene. Afternoon teas, sports, fancy dress and a tug-of-war follow, with the evening being rounded off with a dance. One commentator goes as far as to say that East Brent began the tradition of Harvest Home festivities back in 1857.

Refreshments   The Knoll Inn in East Brent, a short distance from the end of the walk, serves various bar-meals and snacks, as well as offering a beer garden. The top of Brent Knoll would provide an excellent spot for a picnic.

Route 9   4 miles

Westhay Moor and the River Brue

Outline   Westhay ~ Westhay Moor ~ River Brue ~ Westhay.

Summary   The Somerset Levels have been the scene of conflict and strife since time immemorial. The earliest settlers had to do battle against the invading tides and river floodwaters, a battle that was eventually won thanks to the construction of an elaborate network of drainage channels and artificial waterways. Today's conflict is between commercial interests and conservationists. Peat extraction on the Levels necessitates lowering the water-table. This destroys the conditions favoured by the moisture loving plants and creatures for which the region is so well-known. This ramble across Westhay Moor explores an area where a compromise of sorts has been struck. Whilst peat extraction is continuing apace, the exhausted workings have been flooded to create a fine nature reserve. A fascinating 4-mile circuit, in an area where contour lines seem to have been forgotten by the cartographer!

Attractions   Westhay is a small village consisting largely of scattered farms. One of the local farmers, Mr. Ray Sweet, was clearing the ditches on his land in 1970 when he stumbled across pieces of waterlogged timber and a flint arrowhead. Sensing a valuable find, expert archaeological advice was summoned and an ancient trackway was discovered. Subsequently named the Sweet Track, this routeway which dates from 4,000 B.C. is believed to be the world's oldest footpath. Basically, what Ray Sweet had discovered was the remains of a gangway constructed of wooden poles. The construction enabled ancient fisherman and hunters to make their way across what was then a waterlogged landscape. The Willows Garden Centre, on the road from Westhay to Shapwick, houses the Peat Moors Visitors Centre. As well as displays relating to the local peat industry, a mock-up section of the Sweet Way can be seen.

Westhay Moor was described in the Middle Ages as being 'wet and weely, miry and moorish'. This is rather a gloomy picture for a landscape that has more recently been described as 'wild country . . . fascinating and quite magical'. The second description is far closer to the truth! The damp, low-lying peat moor is criss-crossed by a network of drainage ditches, known locally as 'rhynes'. This watery environment provides a natural home for such diverse wildfowl as swans, herons and kingfishers, whilst flocks of peewits are a common sight in the surrounding fields. Part of the exhausted peat working has been purchased by the Somerset Trust

continued on page 46

Route 9

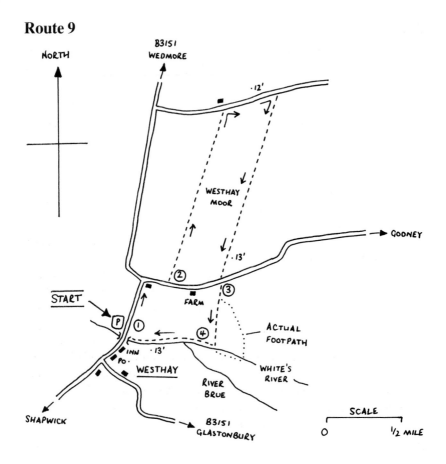

NORTH

B3151
WEDMORE

·12'

WESTHAY
MOOR

·13'

GOONEY

②

START

P

①

③

FARM

④

ACTUAL
FOOTPATH

WHITE'S
RIVER

INN
PO·

·13'

WESTHAY

RIVER
BRUE

SHAPWICK

B3151
GLASTONBURY

SCALE

0   ½ MILE

Route 9

Westhay Moor and the River Brue   4 miles

START   *Westhay lies on the B3151, midway between Glastonbury and Wedmore. On the Wedmore side of the village, there is a parking area alongside Westhay Bridge, where the B3151 crosses the River Brue. The parking area also has a display board giving information about the Somerset Levels. G.R. 438427.*

ROUTE

1. *Walk northwards along the B3151 for just under ½ mile to Turnpike House. Take due care along this relatively busy road, for there are no pavements! At Turnpike House, turn right on to the much quieter Godney road.*

2. *In just 300 yards, turn left on to the drove track that heads northwards across Westhay Moor. In 1¼ miles, the drove joins a quiet lane. Turn right, follow the lane eastwards for 600 yards before turning right on to a parallel drove track that heads back in a southerly direction across the Levels. This return drove passes through extensive peat workings before rejoining the Godney road.*

3. *Directly opposite is a track which is followed due south for almost ½ mile to the north bank of White's River. This is a slight deviation from the actual right-of-way (see map) occasioned by a couple of missing footbridges across the deep and wide drainage channels!*

4. *Follow the north bank of the river back to Westhay Bridge. In a few hundred yards, White's River joins the River Brue.*

Public Transport   Public transport is infrequent and unreliable in this remote part of Central Somerset.

COOT   Black/White forehead   38cm.

45

for Nature Conservation and is being developed as Greater Westhay Reserve. Alder and willow have been planted, and extensive reed beds developed. The Reserve has attracted badgers and foxes, kestrels and coots, as well as large numbers of dragonfly. With such a rich abundance of flora and fauna across the peat moors, a pair of binoculars are an absolute must on this walk.

Peat - vegetable matter decomposed by water and partly carbonised by chemical change - has been worked for many years on the Somerset Levels. It was traditionally hand-dug, and used in local homesteads as a fuel. Peat burning gives off a fragrant aroma. Today, peat extraction is a major business, with the product having a variety of horticultural uses. Cutting machines carve trenches 3 feet deep and 2 feet wide, and the conveniently sized slices of peat are then hand-stacked to facilitate drying. Controversy surrounds the industry, however, with the water table on the moors having to be lowered by pumping to facilitate peat extraction. This destroys the unique habitats in the area, with the conditions favoured by moisture-loving plants being gradually destroyed. Conservationists fear that, at current rates of extraction, the area could become little more than a collection of flooded pits in the ground in the not too distant future. The workings, however, are a fascinating sight, with the neatly stacked lines of peat blocks lying alongside extensive trenches filled with ebony-coloured water. The peat workings have been described as a 'lowland Blaenau Ffestiniog', a not unrealistic description to anyone who has visited this slate-mining town in North Wales!

Refreshments At the end of the walk, just across the River Brue in the village of Westhay, the Bird in Hand public house serves a wide range of bar food.

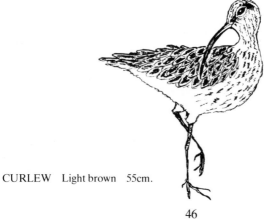

CURLEW   Light brown   55cm.

Glastonbury and the Tor

Outline   Glastonbury ~ Chalice Well ~ Glastonbury Tor ~ Chalice Hill ~ Glastonbury.

Summary   The mystical kingdom of Avalon has traditionally been associated with Glastonbury and its famous Tor. In Celtic legend, Avalon was the 'island of the blest' or 'paradise', whilst in Arthurian legend it was the 'land of heroes' to which the dead king was conveyed. Although no longer surrounded by lake and marshland, the massive hillock rising out of the early morning mist as it blankets the Somerset Levels is indeed reminiscent of a mysterious island silhouetted against the Somerset sky. Despite the lack of miles, the steep ascent of the Tor will ensure that the lungs are fully exercised!

Attractions   Glastonbury is a place of legend. The Glastonbury Thorn that grows on Wearyall Hill and in the Abbey grounds allegedly sprouted from the staff of Joseph of Arimathea, visiting Britain after the Crucifixion; the waters of the Chalice Well flow red because Joseph is said to have deposited the Chalice Cup of the Last Supper beneath its waters . . . although the presence of local iron deposits may be nearer the truth! The bodies of King Arthur and Queen Guinevere are said to repose in the Abbey grounds, with the site of the tomb still commemorated with a plaque, whilst the Tor was supposedly the entrance to the Underworld, the kingdom of Annwn. Certainly, the town acts as a magnet to any number of travelling folk whose beards, beads and balding pates dominate the local high street!

The Tor, with its ruined tower that once belonged to the 14th century St. Michael's Church, has a dominance that belies its mere 520 feet. This is clearly due to it lying amidst the excessively horizontal landscape of the surrounding Levels. From the Tor, a 360 degree panorama over the whole of the Vale of Avalon opens up. To the north rise the Mendip Hills, to the west Brent Knoll and the Bristol Channel, whilst far away in the south-west lie the hills of Exmoor. Amidst such beauty and tranquillity, it is easy to forget that this spot once housed the local gibbet. Abbot Richard Whiting, the last Abbot of Glastonbury, met his end here in 1539, following the Dissolution. His body was quartered, and the citizens of Bath, Wells, Bridgwater and Ilminster were treated to a display of his dismembered parts!

continued on page 50

D   47

Route 10

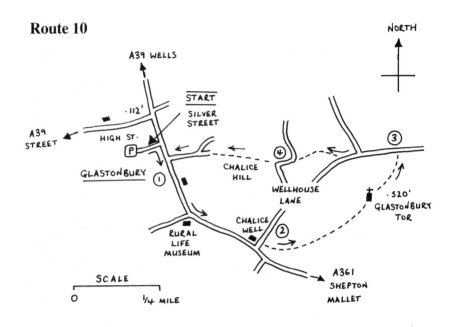

NORTH

A39 WELLS

START
SILVER
STREET

·112'

A39
STREET

HIGH ST·

P

GLASTONBURY

①

RURAL
LIFE
MUSEUM

CHALICE
WELL

CHALICE
HILL

④

WELLHOUSE
LANE

②

③

·520'
GLASTONBURY
TOR

A361
SHEPTON
MALLET

SCALE

0   ¼ MILE

GLASTONBURY TOR

Route 10

Glastonbury and the Tor
2½ miles

START   *Glastonbury lies on the A39 Bath to Minehead road. As you approach the town centre from Wells, rather than bearing right into the High Street, continue straight on along the A361 signposted to Shepton Mallet. Almost immediately, there is a right turn into Silver Street where you will find a local authority car-park. G.R. 502389.*

ROUTE

1. *Return to the main road - Chilkwell Street - turn right and continue to the junction with Bere Lane, opposite the Rural Life Museum. Turn left at this busy junction and continue for 400 yards to Wellhouse Lane.*

2. *Just a short distance along Wellhouse Lane, turn right to follow the signposted footpath to the Tor. Follow the obvious route to the hilltop, where you will undoubtedly pause to enjoy one of the finest views in Somerset. Descend the far-side of the Tor by another obvious path to rejoin Wellhouse Lane.*

3. *Turn left at Wellhouse Lane and, in 400 yards, look out for a stile on the right-hand side. Cross this stile and bear half-left to reach a second clearly visible stile. Follow the right-hand hedgerow beyond this stile on to Lypyatt Lane.*

4. *Ahead, the lane bears sharply to the left. At this point, continue straight on along a footpath that descends Chalice Hill before joining Dod Lane. Continue down Dod Lane to rejoin Chilkwell Street, turn right and it is but a few yards to Silver Street.*

Public Transport Badgerline operate several services in the Glastonbury area, including a regular Bristol to Yeovil route that passes through the town.

The Abbey Barn, the 14th century home barn of Glastonbury Abbey, has been open to the public since 1976 as the home of the Somerset Rural Life Museum. The complex also includes the adjoining Victorian farmhouse. The barn's interior roof structure, described by experts as 'two-tier cruck design', vividly displays the skills of the medieval carpenter. Following its restoration, this fine structure - 93 feet long and 33 feet wide - was reroofed in mellow Cotswold stone. The museum's displays focus on 19th and early 20th century social, domestic and agricultural activities, whilst one fascinating exhibition documents the life story of a local farm-labourer, John Hodges of Butleigh, from cradle to grave.

Refreshments In Glastonbury, there are many inns, cafes and tea-shops. If you prefer a packed lunch, there can be few better picnicking spots than the Tor.

TOOTLE BRIDGE

Route 11   4 miles
Baltonsborough and the River Brue

Outline   Baltonsborough ~ River Brue ~ Tootle Bridge ~ Catsham ~ Baltonsborough.

Summary   It is difficult to explore the countryside around Glastonbury without being confronted by one or other of the great characters of English history. Whilst Alfred and Arthur are but the most well-known, second division heroes are almost two-a-penny! At Baltonsborough, the local boy-made-good is Dunstan. A one-time Abbot of Glastonbury, he later rose to even greater prominence as Archbishop of Canterbury. Perhaps surprisingly for a cleric, Dunstan was immensely practical. His skills ensured that the low-lying land around his birthplace was adequately drained by the River Brue. In addition, he developed an extensive mill-stream for the village. This ramble explores the level countryside around Baltonsborough, following in Dunstan's footsteps along the banks of the Brue to Tootle Bridge, before returning by way of the mill-stream to the parish church of Saint Dunstan's. A truly pleasant waterside stroll.

Attractions   St. Dunstan was born at Baltonsborough in the early years of the 10th century. As a young man, he won favour with King Athelstan, soothing the troubled brow of the sovereign with his musical abilities. Soon, however, he was to forsake the pleasure of the flesh by entering the strict regime of Glastonbury Abbey. Here he constructed a hermit's cell for himself that measured a mere 5 feet by 2½ feet! The devil ill-advisedly visited Dunstan on one occasion in an attempt to lure him away from his pious lifestyle, only to have his nose tweaked by a set of red-hot tongs . . . at least, that is the story portrayed on the banner in Baltonsborough Church! By 940 A.D., the zealous Dunstan had become Abbot of Glastonbury, while just 19 years later he had risen to the venerable rank of Archbishop of Canterbury. Dunstan's birthplace was at Ham Street, a mile east of the village centre, where a commemorative memorial of Doulting limestone has been erected.

The River Brue is truly a Somerset river, rising on the county's eastern border above Bruton, before flowing past Glastonbury and Meare to join the Bristol Channel at Burnham-on-Sea. Around Baltonsborough, the low-lying farmland used to be flooded repeatedly as the Brue sprawled over its banks following heavy rainfall. With Baltonsborough being one of the twelve manors of Glastonbury Abbey,

continued on page 54

51

Route 11

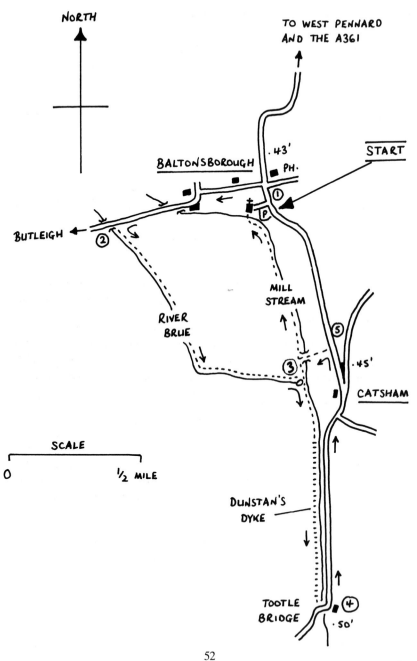

NORTH

TO WEST PENNARD
AND THE A361

START

BALTONSBOROUGH

·43'

PH.

BUTLEIGH

①

②

P

MILL
STREAM

RIVER
BRUE

⑤

③

·45'

CATSHAM

SCALE

0   ½ MILE

DUNSTAN'S
DYKE

TOOTLE
BRIDGE

④

·50'

52

Route 11

Baltonsborough and the River Brue   4 miles

START   *West Pennard lies 3 miles east of Glastonbury on the A361 to Shepton Mallet. As you enter the village from Glastonbury, a turning on the right is signposted to Baltonsborough. 2 miles of driving along minor roads will bring you to the village. There is room for parking in Church Walk, a cul-de-sac lane on the right-hand side just past the Greyhound Public House. G.R. 543348.*

ROUTE

1. *Return to the main road, turn left and walk 100 yards to the crossroads alongside the Greyhound P.H. Turn left, and follow the road signposted to Butleigh and Street. In a little over ½ mile, after passing Mill Farm, the Mill and the Gatehouse, you will reach Wallyer's Bridge and the River Brue.*

2. *Turn left into the field that lies alongside the Baltonsborough bank of the river. Follow this north bank of the Brue for a little over ½ mile to its confluence with the Baltonsborough Mill Stream.*

3. *Cross the Brue by means of the footbridge, and continue following the river bank in a southerly direction for 1 mile to Tootle Bridge. This section of the footpath follows a raised bank named Dunstan's Dyke.*

4. *Cross Tootle Bridge and follow the quiet lane northwards alongside the Brue. In just over ½ mile, the lane heads away from the river bank.*

5. *In less than ½ mile, after a couple of road junctions where the left-hand option is followed, a track heads off on the left-hand side. Follow this track down to the Mill Stream, cross the stream and turn right. Follow the banks of this quiet water-course back to Baltonsborough Church.*

Public Transport   Badgerline Buses operate a service from Glastonbury to Somerton that passes through Baltonsborough.

Dunstan put his practical skills to full use by excavating a deep ditch for the river to follow from Tootle Bridge to Catsham. This effectively put an end to this localised flooding, with no doubt an increase following in agricultural productivity in this corner of the Abbey's landholdings. The river channel is now known quite appropriately as Dunstan's Dyke. At the same time, Dunstan created a series of weirs on the Brue to ensure an efficient supply of water into Baltonsborough's mill-stream, an undoubted series of achievements for a mystic!

Tootle Bridge is a site of some intrigue. On its southern supports, the bowl or depression is reputedly a built-in font. Indeed, this is believed to be the very spot where Dunstan himself was christened. A more touching tale, however, relates to a drunk who 'overspilled himself' from the bridge one dark night in the last century. He landed upside down in the font, his head firmly wedged under the holy waters, and was found dead the following morning!

St. Dunstan's Church is unusual insofar as the whole fabric is of a uniform date. The current building dates back to the 15th century. Perhaps the most fascinating feature within the building is a strange Jacobean hinged seat, attached to one end of a pew. Its purpose is unknown - maybe it was a baby seat, perhaps it was a 'maid's stool', it could even have been a 'seat of penance'. Another mystery concerns a ghostly monk who is said to visit the churchyard. Locally associated with Dunstan, the village children have been taught to believe that he will appear if they run nine times around the outside of the church. The beauty with such a tale is the opportunity it provides for youngsters to burn-off any excess energy they might still possess at the end of this ramble!

Refreshments   The Greyhound Inn in Baltonsborough can offer drinks and light snacks. The banks of the Brue provide many excellent spots for a picnic.

CORMORANT   Dark brown   90cm.

Huntspill and Bridgwater Bay

Outline Huntspill ~ River Brue ~ Parrett Estuary ~ Huntspill River ~ Huntspill.

Summary River estuaries provide a fascinating environment where fresh and salt water combine to form a brackish water, an ever-changing mixture of salt, mud and sand. Bridgwater Bay, where the Parrett and the Brue discharge their waters into the Bristol Channel, is an excellent example of such an environment. The mud flats support a complex food chain, culminating in the large number of birds that feed upon the abundant supply of mud-dwelling animals. This level circuit overlooking the Bay provides a fascinating glimpse into the natural history of one of Britain's best know mud flats, created as long ago as 1954 by agreement with the Somerset River Board.

Attractions Huntspill is a disorganised collection of cottages, farms and modern houses spread out along a ½ mile stretch of quiet road just to the west of the A38. Prior to 1800, there was no village of Huntspill as such, rather there was just a group of lonely hamlets such as Batts Bow, Cote and Dotts. The modern community is focussed on the 15th century St. Peter's Church. Perhaps rather oddly, a feature of the church is its churchyard railings, described by one commentator as 'having a crispness that marks the fascinating watershed between the Classical of the 18th century and the Gothic of the 19th century'. The railings themselves were forged at Coalbrookdale, the cradle of the Industrial Revolution. Within the church, the red-stained pillars and the cracked shield adorning an effigy of a knight are the reminders of a fierce blaze that savaged the building on the 9th December 1878.

The walk follows the mouths of three of Somerset's better known waterways - the Brue, the Parrett and the Huntspill River - as they flow into Bridgwater Bay. The absolutely straight course of the Huntspill River is testimony to its man-made origins. This vast artificial channel had been proposed as early as 1797 by John Billingsley who farmed at Sutton Mallet. Drainage of the Levels would increase the acreage of productive land, and boost landowners' profits. Finance for such a major capital project was a stumbling block, however, and despite the existence of detailed plans the project did not come to fruition until 1939. Ironically, the construction of the Huntspill River owed nothing to land drainage. A secret munitions factory was being constructed at nearby

continued on page 58

Route 12

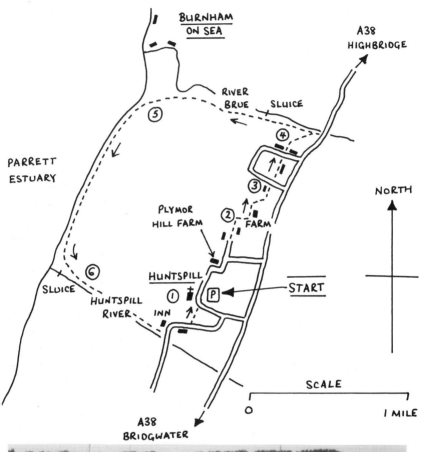

BURNHAM
ON SEA

A38
HIGHBRIDGE

RIVER
BRUE   SLUICE

⑤

④

PARRETT
ESTUARY

NORTH

③

PLYMOR
HILL FARM

②   FARM

⑥

SLUICE

HUNTSPILL
RIVER

HUNTSPILL

①

INN

🅿   START

A38
BRIDGWATER

SCALE

O   1 MILE

BRUE ESTUARY

Route 12

Huntspill and Bridgwater Bay

5 miles

START   *West Huntspill lies just ½ mile to the west of the A38, 7 miles north of Bridgwater. Heading north from Bridgwater, the left turn into the village is just north of the Huntspill River. Park carefully on the road adjacent to St. Peter's Church. G.R. 304454.*

ROUTE

1. *Follow the road northwards through the village until, 100 yards past Plymor Hill Farm, the road bears sharply to the right to rejoin the A38. At this point, continue straight ahead along Longlands Lane, which eventually becomes an enclosed path. This path ends at a gateway leading into an open field.*

2. *Follow the right-hand field boundary for 100 yards, before turning right at a gate to follow a concrete path towards some farm buildings. Turn left and walk along close to the back of these farm buildings, continue along the hedgerow beyond and, where this hedgerow ends, cross the open field ahead to a footbridge across a drainage ditch.*

3. *Beyond this footbridge, follow the right-hand field boundary to a stile in the corner of the field. Follow the enclosed path beyond this stile on to a road, follow the path as it continues in the same direction on the opposite side of the road, passing to the rear of some bungalows. The path crosses another road before passing between a pair of houses to enter an open field.*

4. *Cross this field to reach the south bank of the River Brue. Turn left at the river and follow its course to a pair of sluice gates. Beyond these gates, follow the raised bank (i.e. the sea defences) as the Brue heads towards Bridgwater Bay.*

5. *The defences bear southwards and the path is now bordering the mouth of the River Parrett. In just 1 mile, you will reach the sluice gates at the mouth of the Huntspill River.*

6. *Follow the Huntspill River for ¾ mile to Slowy Bridge, either following the actual river bank or the Water Board's access road. Turn left at Slowy Bridge, and follow the country lane past Laburnum House to a rank of cottages. Opposite the last cottage, a gap in the hedgerow on your left brings you into an open field. Head straight across this field to a footbridge and an adjoining kissing gate. Beyond the kissing gate is the Church of St. Peter and the end of your walk.*

Puriton, whose appetite for water was to run to some 3½ million gallons each day. The 5 mile long Huntspill River, running from the South Drain near Burtle to the Parrett Estuary, was literally a linear reservoir. For most locals, however, the Huntspill River is better known as an excellent coarse fishing water. Each weekend, dozens of anglers line the banks in search of 'the one that got away'.

The Bridgwater Bay Nature Reserve runs from Hinkley Point in the west to Stert Island just below Burnham-on-Sea. The coastline in the area is low-lying and dominated by the vast mud flats that appear at low tide. A site of some 6,200 acres, this is an ornithologist's paradise, where a pair of field glasses are an essential companion. Waders are the dominant bird species, with up to 10,000 dunlins inhabiting the Bay in mid-winter. The dunlin's winter companions include redshank and knot, grey plover and oystercatcher. The section of the walk along the muddy banks of the Parrett Estuary provides the best view across the Bay on this particular circuit. The sight of hundreds of dunlin turning and twisting in flight across the mud flats at sunset is an unforgettable experience, provided that the Bay is not being swept by a biting north wind!

N.B. A month-by-month guide to the wildfowl of Bridgwater Bay can be found in Ken Hall's 'Where to watch birds in Somerset, Avon, Gloucestershire and Wiltshire' published by Helm.

Refreshments Laburnum House near the end of the walk (see map) serves a selection of bar snacks as well as cream teas.

Public Transport The Burnham to Bridgwater service operated by Badgerline Buses runs along the A38 just ½ mile from the start of the walk.

Moorlinch and the Polden Hills

Outline   Sutton Mallet ~ Pit Hill ~ Moorlinch ~ Sedgemoor ~ Sutton Mallet.

Summary   The Polden Hills run across Central Somerset from Puriton to Street, never more than a couple of miles wide and acting as a spine that carries the A39 road from Bridgwater eastwards. The Poldens neatly divide the Levels into two parts, with the Vale of Avalon and Glastonbury to the north, and Sedgemoor to the south. Although rising to just 322 feet in height, the Polden Hills bring far-ranging views across the Somerset Levels. This gentle excursion explores the southern slopes of the hills, overlooking King's Sedge Moor and Westonzoyland.

Attractions   Sutton Mallet is little more than an isolated hamlet lying a mile or two south of the A39. There is a church, but the notice in the porch explaining about the 'Redundant Churches Fund' is indicative of its spiritual state today. Internally, the church possesses a fine collection of high box pews, overlooked by a three-decker pulpit. The box pews were by tradition allocated to local farms. Agriculture is the chief concern of Sutton Mallet, the village being essentially a group of half a dozen farms. The 1:25,000 O.S. sheet shows these farms clearly grouped around the village church, and an interesting selection of names they possess including the most un-Somerset 'Nino's Farm'. Any youngster armed with the 'I-Spy On The Farm' booklet would soon be notching-up many valuable points, especially in the farm machinery section, with tractors, bailers, muck-spreaders and the like littering the many farmyards hereabouts.

The 2 mile long bridlepath across Pit Hill to Moorlinch, perched some 75 feet above Sedgemoor, is an all-too-rare enclosed green lane. Throughout Britain, hedgerows are a fast disappearing part of the landscape as farmers seek to increase their field sizes. The importance of a hedgerow is its role in the food chain, where it provides the staple diet of any number of insects that in turn support the local bird and animal population. Hedgerows can be dated by the number of mature trees and shrubs that they contain, each species representing approximately 100 years in the age of the hedgerow. In the hedges bordering this bridlepath, you should be able to spot at least 10 different species, including crab-apple, blackthorn and elder. This dates these hedgerows to at least 800 A.D., if not earlier. Unfortunately, with a J.C.B., they can disappear in just minutes!

continued on page 62

Route 13

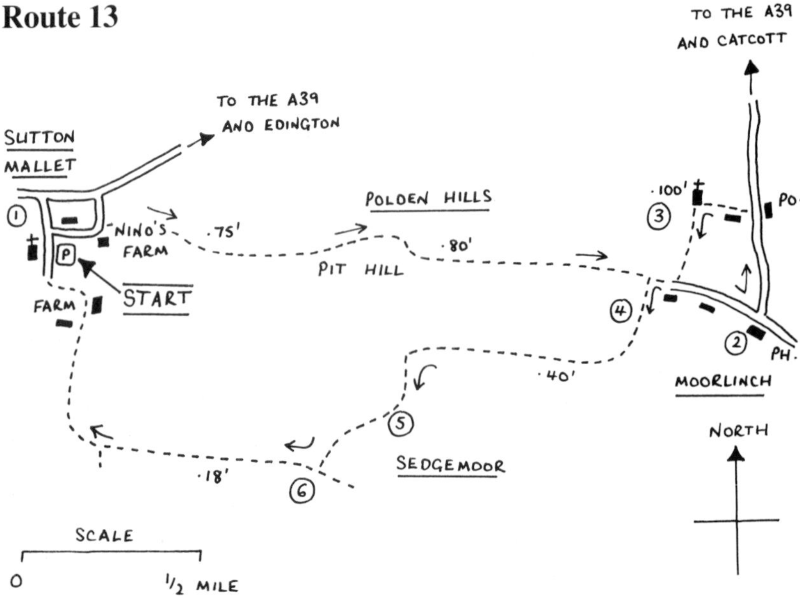

TO THE A39
AND CATCOTT

SUTTON
MALLET

TO THE A39
AND EDINGTON

POLDEN HILLS

·100'

PO·

NINO'S
FARM

·75'

PIT HILL

·80'

③

①

START

④

②

PH·

FARM

MOORLINCH

·40'

NORTH

⑤

·18'

SEDGEMOOR

⑥

SCALE

0   ½ MILE

SEDGEMOOR

60

Route 13

Moorlinch and the Polden Hills
4½ miles

START   *The A39 Bridgwater to Street road runs across the ridge of the Polden Hills. 6 miles east of Bridgwater, turn off on to the minor road signposted to Sutton Mallet. In this small village, park alongside the now redundant church. G.R. 373369.*

ROUTE

1. *Follow the road back in the direction of the A39 (see map). Where it bears to the left alongside Nino's Farm, continue straight ahead along a bridlepath. Follow this wide, enclosed path, slightly elevated above Sedgemoor, for 2 miles until you reach the Ring O Bells Inn at Moorlinch.*

2. *At the Ring O Bells, turn left and follow the main road uphill for 200 yards until, on the right-hand side, you find the village stores and post-office. At this point, turn left on to a gravelled drive that leads to Moorlinch Church.*

3. *From the church porch, descend to the kissing gate in the bottom right-hand corner of the churchyard. Follow the edge of the field beyond this kissing gate downhill to rejoin the bridlepath that leads back to Sutton Mallet. (For an easy return to Sutton Mallet, simply retrace your steps along this bridlepath).*

4. *Turn right, and in ¼ mile fork left off the main path on to another enclosed track. Follow this track for 1 mile, along the flat, northern edge of Sedgemoor, until you emerge into an open field.*

5. *Bear right to the far corner of this field, 20 yards to the left of a telegraph pole. In the next field, aim for the far left-hand corner where you will join a drove track with extensive views to the south across Sedgemoor.*

6. *Follow this track to the right for over ½ mile, where it bears to the right to climb uphill back into Sutton Mallet. You will pass a complex of farm buildings before you arrive back at the village church.*

Public Transport   Whilst Sutton Mallet is not served by a bus service, the Street to Bridgwater service does pass through Edington, 2 miles to the north. This route is operated by Badgerline buses.

Moorlinch has been described as 'sunny and south-facing, with cottages clinging limpet-like to the steep road', a very apt description of its most attractive location. The study of place-names produces an interesting insight into the character of the village. The 'moor' is derived from 'mirie' meaning merry or happy, whilst the 'linch' is drawn from 'lynchets', cultivation terraces that were developed on the local hillsides. The 'merry hillside' is the consequent translation placed on the name by one local authority! Before Sedgemoor was drained, the village would have looked down upon a marsh estuary, and the local population would have included numbers of fishermen. Their boats would have been hauled up on to the slopes each evening, as the catches of fish were brought ashore to be sold at the Fish Cross in the village. The church is perched on the hillside above the village, providing what Pevsner described as 'a view not easily forgotten'. This epitaph was certainly true in July 1685, when the villagers gathered on the hill to witness the battle being fought at nearby Westonzoyland. Some of the defeated soldiers actually beat a retreat through Moorlinch from what was the last battle to be fought in England.

Refreshments Conveniently situated half way around the walk in Moorlinch is the Ring O Bells Inn.

BATTLE OF SEDGEMOOR MEMORIAL

Westonzoyland and King's Sedgemoor Drain

Outline   Westonzoyland ~ Bussex Farm ~ King's Sedgemoor Drain ~ Parchey Bridge ~ Bussex Farm ~ Westonzoyland.

Summary   The flat, lonely fields to the north of Westonzoyland were the site of the Battle of Sedgemoor, the last battle to be fought on English soil. This was an attempt by the Western Rebellion, an ill-equipped and untrained army of peasants, to overthrow King Charles II's brother James. This ramble explores the battlefield site, as well as a network of drove tracks, some of which were undoubtedly used by the rebel army to reach Westonzoyland from Bridgwater. On those cold autumnal mornings, when the mists envelope Sedgemoor, the imaginative mind can easily recreate the scene of July 6th 1685. The ghostly shapes in the distance - in all probability nothing more than a herd of friesian cows - could well be Monmouth's rebels stealing across the moors under cover of darkness!

Attractions   Following the death of King Charles II in 1685, his brother James succeeded him to the throne. He was deeply unpopular, and it was not long before his reign was challenged. Charles II's illegitimate son, the Duke of Monmouth, landed in Lyme Regis from Holland and established the Western Rebellion. This was essentially a peasant army, brave but poorly armed, that was described as being 'tactically bankrupt'. By Sunday 5th July 1685, Monmouth and 3,500 men were cornered in Bridgwater by the Royal army. A villager from nearby Chedzoy offered to guide the rebels under cover of darkness across the moors to Westonzoyland, where the intention was to give the King's army an almighty surprise. The plan was successful until the rebel army lost its way on the marshes, confusion arose, a stray pistol shot was sounded and the King's army were unfortunately alerted. The peasant army were routed, being 'shot, hung and hacked without mercy'. The few survivors were herded like cattle into Westonzoyland Church, where they were held until the Bloody Assize. The rebels received a severe punishment - some were executed, some transported to Barbados, others merely whipped. On the battlefield site, a monument was erected in 1928. It reads:

> 'To the glory of God and in memory of all who, doing right as they saw it, fell in the Battle of Sedgemoor, 6th July 1685, and lie buried in this field or for their share in the fight suffered death, punishment or transportation'.

continued on page 66

Route 14

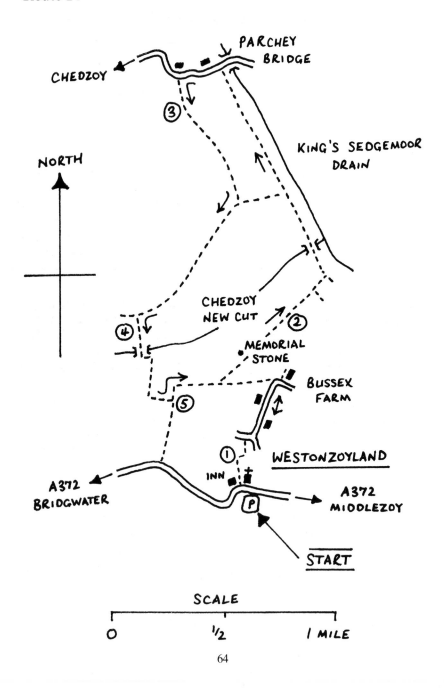

PARCHEY BRIDGE

CHEDZOY

③

NORTH

KING'S SEDGEMOOR DRAIN

CHEDZOY NEW CUT

④

②

MEMORIAL STONE

⑤

BUSSEX FARM

①

WESTONZOYLAND

A372 BRIDGWATER

INN

P

A372 MIDDLEZOY

START

SCALE

O   ½   1 MILE

64

Route 14

Westonzoyland and King's Sedgemoor Drain   4½ miles

START *Westonzoyland lies midway between Bridgwater and Middlezoy on the A372. There is room for roadside parking on the main A372 alongside St. Mary the Virgin Church in the centre of the village. G.R. 352348.*

ROUTE

1. *Head northwards along Church Lane, the lane that runs to the west of the church. Where the road bears to the right in front of Church Cottage, continue straight ahead along the public footpath. The path passes the backs of several bungalows before it joins Monmouth Road. Turn right and follow Monmouth Road northwards to Bussex Farm, where a left turn on to a drove track brings you into the flat open countryside of Sedgemoor. In just 300 yards, turn right on to another track, that will soon bring you to the memorial stone erected to commemorate the Battle of Sedgemoor.*

2. *Continue along this drove for ½ mile to a point where it bears sharply to the right. Ignore this right turn, instead continue straight ahead through a gateway and on to the south bank of Kings Sedgemoor Drain. Turn left, follow the Drain for 1 mile to Parchey Bridge, and turn left at the Chedzoy road. In just 200 yards, turn left opposite Parchey Cottage on to a drove track.*

3. *Follow this track for ½ mile to a junction where you bear right on to another drove track. Continue along this track until you come to the fifth gateway on the left past the electricity pylons. The gateway is marked with a yellow arrow, and is shortly before the track bears off to the right.*

4. *Follow the edge of the field beyond this gateway, alongside a hedge, on to a footbridge across Chedzoy New Cut. In the field beyond the Cut, follow the left-hand field boundaries until you reach the far left-hand corner of the field. Here you turn left along a track.*

5. *Shortly you will come to a junction. Turn left and follow the track back to Bussex Farm. It is now simply a question of retracing your steps to Westonzoyland church.*

Public Transport   Badgerline Buses operate a regular service between Bridgwater and Westonzoyland.

Somerset is renowned for churches of the Perpendicular style, and St. Mary the Virgin at Westonzoyland is no exception. The Perpendicular period of church architecture dated from 1400 to 1500, and it is the sheer 'uprightness' of its churches that is immediately recognisable. It was to St. Mary's that 500 captured rebels were taken following the Battle of Sedgemoor. The church records tell us that 79 of these prisoners were wounded, 5 of whom died of their wounds within the church. It is a shame that these prisoners were in such a poor state of health and mind, for had they the strength to raise their eyes, they would have glimpsed one of the finest timber roofs in the country. It has been described as the 'triumph of the church', being splendidly carved with angels and decorative bosses. The churchwarden's account book for 1685 carries a particularly poignant entry:

'Paid for ffrankinsenssense and peivey and reffon and other things to burn in the church after ye prisoners was gone out;
5 shillings 8 pence'.

King's Sedgemoor Drain is an artificial channel cut to divert the waters of the River Cary away from those of the Parrett. Following heavy rainfall, these two great Somerset rivers were responsible for some of the worst flooding on the Levels, a situation described by one 18th century observer as 'a discredit to so fine a county'. After many years of discussion, a vast channel was eventually dug to carry the waters of the River Cary from Henley Corner, below High Ham, the 12 miles to Dunball on the Parrett estuary. The grandiose project was given the Royal Assent in 1791, and cost the princely sum of £31,600 to undertake. The Drain is a haven for wildfowl, with mute swans being the most majestic residents. The adult male is the largest British bird, weighing upwards of 20 pounds and measuring an incredible 5 feet from beak to tail! 'Mute' is perhaps a wholly inappropriate adjective to apply to these fine birds, for they often snort, hiss and call quite dramatically, as well as issuing the legendary 'swan song' shortly before their death.

Refreshments The Sedgemoor Inn lies just along the road from St. Mary the Virgin Church at the end of the walk in Westonzoyland. This hostelry serves a wide range of drinks and refreshments.

High Ham, the River Cary and Stembridge Tower Mill

Outline   High Ham ~ Turn Hill ~ Henley Corner ~ the River Cary ~ Stembridge Tower Mill ~ High Ham.

Summary   A relatively long circuit in and around the village of High Ham, where the landscape is typical of much of Central Somerset - an area of high ground rising up from what was formerly damp, low-lying marshland. The high ground is best typified by the National Trust's Turn Hill property, an excellent viewpoint across King's Sedge Moor, whilst on the low ground, the circuit follows a network of rhynes, drainage ditches and rivers. At the end of the walk, Stembridge Tower Mill provides a suitable finale to a circuit that is never short of interest.

Attractions   The centre of High Ham village presents a scene that post-card manufacturers must just dream of! A tree-lined village green, surrounded by all those ever-so English buildings - the almshouses, an old school house, a former rectory, fine cottages and, of course, the parish church. Fortunately, High Ham is very much off the beaten track, and its delights have remained virtually unrecognised. The church possesses a fine collection of gargoyles, including a group of musicians who appear to be creating such a cacophony of sound that a neighbouring carved figure is cringing with pain! To the west of the village lies Turn Hill, a N.T. property that provides a fine viewpoint across King's Sedge Moor, some 300 feet below. The view seems never-ending as a patchwork of fields stretch away into the distant haze, interspersed with some of the finest church towers anywhere in England. Try and take a 1:50,000 O.S. sheet with you - and attempt to pick-out the more obvious landmarks that include the churches at Chedzoy, Othery, Middlezoy and Westonzoyland.

Between Charity Farm and Henley Corner - provided that you are following the more strenuous of the two suggested routes - the path follows the course of the Old River Cary. Prior to the 18th century, the Rivers Cary and Parrett ran in close proximity through much of Central Somerset. To alleviate the flooding that this often caused, and to assist in the drainage of the Levels, the Cary's waters were diverted into a vast artificial channel - Kings Sedge Moor Drain. Henley Bridge marks the point where the Cary was diverted, leaving its former course resembling an overgrown drainage channel. East of Henley Bridge, we are walking a

continued on page 70

Route 15

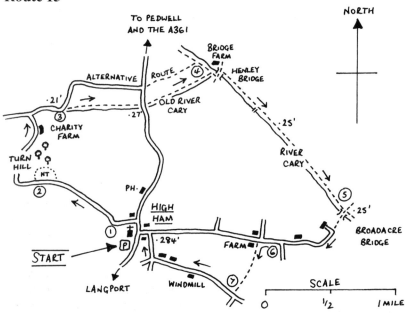

SWAN FAMILY, RIVER CARY

Route 15   7 miles

High Ham, the River Cary and Stembridge Tower Mill

START   *4 miles west of Street, the A361 Taunton road leaves the A39 Bridgwater road. Follow the A361 for just 1 mile to Pedwell, where you turn left on to the minor road signposted to High Ham. It is just 4 miles to the village, where there is ample room for parking on the village green, directly opposite the church. G.R. 426311.*

ROUTE

1. *From the village green, turn left in front of South View House to follow the lane that passes behind the church. In a little over ½ mile, you will reach Turn Hill, a National Trust property. It is worth making a detour off of the road to the fine vantage point that overlooks the moors below.*

2. *Continue down the hill, following the lane, until you reach a T-junction a short distance beyond Charity Farm. Turn right, and follow the lane for ¼ mile until it bears sharply to the left.*

3. *Immediately ahead is a gateway. Cross the gate, and follow the small drainage ditch on your right for over ½ mile until you reach High Ham road. This ditch is in fact the old course of the River Cary. Cross the road, and continue following the same ditch eastwards until it joins the modern-day course of the Cary.*

N.B.   *In summer months, the above route is rather overgrown with nettles and difficult to negotiate. The alternative route - shown on the map - is somewhat easier if less exciting!*

4. *Turn right when you reach the south bank of the Cary. Almost immediately, cross the river by means of Henley Bridge, turn right and continue following the north bank of the river.*

5. *In 1½ miles, leave the river-bank at Broadacre Bridge, the third bridge on from Henley Bridge. Cross the river, and follow the lane beyond past Lower and Higher Broadacre Farms and on to a road junction. Follow the road to the right for 200 yards until you reach Stout Farm.*

6. *Turn left on to the track immediately before the farm buildings. Almost straightaway, cross the gate ahead and follow the right-hand hedgerow uphill in the field beyond. Where the hedge ends, continue uphill in the same direction to a stile in the hedgerow ahead. Bear half-left in the next field to a second stile underneath an ash tree in the opposite hedgerow. Follow the direction indicated by the yellow arrow on this stile i.e. gradually downhill and to the left. This soon brings you out on to a quiet lane.*

7. *Turn right, follow the lane uphill until you come to Stembridge Tower Mill. Continue along the road for ¼ mile beyond the mill, where the first turning on the right - just beyond a row of houses - will return you to the village green in High Ham.*

Public Transport   High Ham is on the road from nowhere to nowhere - public transport is therefore non-existent!

---

stretch of the 'genuine' River Cary, with a rather special selection of wildfowl. Swans, herons and kingfishers are but three of the fascinating species to keep your eyes open for.

In the past, open and exposed hillsides provided perfect locations for windmills. The slopes of High Ham Hill were no exception, and it comes as no surprise to find Stembridge Tower Mill on the edge of High Ham village. A tower mill is capped-out with a revolving turret, and has a fantail to ensure that the sails are always pointing windward. Stembridge is, in fact, the last remaining thatched windmill in England. It dates from 1822, and was in use until 1910. The mill is now a N.T. property, and is open to the public on a selection of summer afternoons. If you wish to ensure that your walk coincides with the mill's opening, then you should phone Langport (0458) 250818 for information.

Refreshments   The Kings Head Inn, just a short distance from the end of the walk (see map), can supply ample refreshment at the end of this ramble.

BURROW MUMP

Burrow Mump and Southlake Moor

Outline Burrow Mump ~ Burrowbridge ~ River Parrett ~ Sowy River ~ Earlake Moor ~ Burrowbridge ~ Burrow Mump.

Summary Burrow Mump, although a mere 75 feet in height, dominates much of Sedgemoor just as Glastonbury Tor overshadows the Vale of Avalon. Both are isolated hillocks adorned with ecclesiastical ruins, where a tremendous sense of history pervades the atmosphere. This level circuit explores the rivers and rhynes, the moors and the settlements around the Mump. The climax to the walk will undoubtedly be the final ascent of Burrow Mump, from where an unrivalled 360° panorama of Sedgemoor is obtained. With such a fine view in prospect, it is imperative to pick a fine and clear day for this particular ramble.

Attractions The Isle of Athelney, an area of firm ground that rises out of what was formerly marshland, will always be associated with King Alfred. It was here in A.D. 878 that he established his headquarters when hiding from the Danes, in a setting that gave birth to the legend of the burnt cakes. Just a mile to the north-east of Athelney is the 75 foot hillock of Burrow Mump, another island that rose out of the marshes of Sedgemoor back in the 9th century. The Mump was a look-out post in those distant times, standing guard over the River Parrett and the approach to Alfred's headquarters. The ruined chapel at its summit is dedicated to St. Michael, although excavations have revealed earlier buildings on the site, including a Norman building that may have been a castle.

To the east of Burrow Mump stretches the vastness of Southlake Moor. This is one surviving area of the Levels where traditional winter flooding occurs to this day, forming a huge lake throughout much of the winter season. The flooding is carried out under the auspices of the Somerset Trust for Nature Conservation, whose chief concern is to maintain a damp habitat for the large numbers of waders - lapwing, snipe, redshank and curlew - that thrive in the area. Modern drainage techniques have lowered the water-table beneath the Levels and have threatened to destroy so much of its unique character. The flooding has an added benefit insofar as it spreads rich river sediment across the local fields, providing a natural source of fertilizer for farmers. Ironically, the embankments or 'walls' that were originally built to assist in the drainage of Southlake Moor, today contain its winter flood waters and prevent them for invading the surrounding roads and villages.

continued on page 74

Route 16

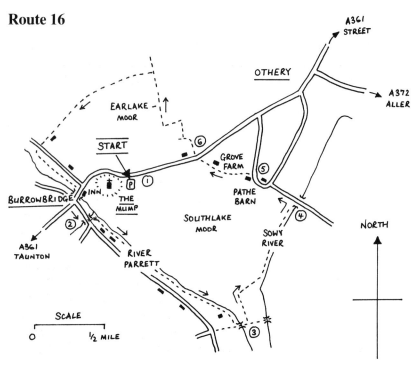

BURROW MUMP

Route 16

Burrow Mump and Southlake Moor   6 miles

START   *The A361 Taunton to Street road passes through Burrowbridge, where the Mump is a prominent feature for miles around. At the eastern end of Burrow Mump, just alongside the main road, is a car-park for visitors to this National Trust property. G.R. 360305.*

ROUTE

1. *Cross the stile into the N.T. Burrow Mump property, and follow the right-hand hedgerow to the far side of the hill. In the corner of the enclosure, a kissing gate and some steps bring you on to the busy A361 road through Burrowbridge. Continue along the A361, past the King Alfred Inn, across the Parrett, and then turn left on to the Athelney and Stoke St. Gregory road. In 300 yards the road crosses the River Tone, just below its confluence with the Parrett.*

2. *Once across the Tone, turn left through a gateway to reach the river bank. Follow the Tone the few yards to its confluence with the Parrett, and there turn right to follow the banks of the Parrett upstream for 1½ miles until you reach a bridge where you cross to the far bank of the river. (If the river bank path is closed for any reason, an alternative route along the lanes can be followed to the same point — see map).*

3. *Once across the Parrett, turn immediately left through a gateway and head across the field beyond to another gate. From this second gateway, bear right to join the banks of the Sowy River, an artificial flood relief channel. Follow the Sowy downstream for ¾ mile to the Pathe to Aller road.*

4. *Turn left at this road, and left again at the junction some 300 yards ahead. Continue along quiet lanes for a short distance until, on the left-hand side, you reach Pathe Barn. Just past this converted farm building, turn left on to a gravelled drive.*

5. *Cross the gate directly ahead and, in the next field, descend the 50 yards to another gate in the bottom left-hand corner. Follow the right-hand hedgerow through the next two fields until you reach Grove Farm. Directly ahead is another gateway - follow the left-hand hedgerow beyond this gate to one final gateway and a track. Turn right at the track to join the A361.*

N.B.   *This section of the walk is not clearly waymarked and a barbed-wire fence obstructs the path at one point. The local authority have been asked to improve the access.*

6. *Cross the A361 and follow the bridlepath opposite, alongside some farm buildings and out on to Earlake Moor. In 200 yards, by a rhyne, the route bears to the right (i.e. ignore the track directly ahead). In another 200 yards, the path bears sharply to the left, whilst in another 200 yards it bears to the right. Continue ahead for ½ mile until you reach the second drove track on your left-hand side - Burrow Drove. Follow this drove for close on 1 mile to a lane that runs alongside the Parrett. Turn left and in just ¼ mile you will arrive back in the middle of Burrowbridge. Turn left at the main road and retrace your steps to the car-park.*

Public Transport Western National Buses operate a service between Taunton and Glastonbury that passes through Burrowbridge.

––––––––––

The River Parrett, our constant companion throughout the earlier stage of the walk, rises just over the Dorset border in South Perrot. The lower reaches of the river below Langport are tidal, and in centuries past acted as an important navigation for much of Central Somerset. The incoming cargoes would have included coal, slate, salt and bricks, whilst out of the region would have flowed elm timber, willow, flax and cider. With the Tone, navigable to Taunton, joining the Parrett at Burrowbridge, this small village beneath Burrow Mump would have been a thriving inland port. Unfortunately, no evidence of this activity exists today.

Until 1946, a toll had to be paid to cross the Parrett at Burrowbridge. The rights to extract this toll from passing traffic were put out to auction on February 10th each year. A complicated bid system operated against the time constraint of a sandglass, with the only stipulation being that the bids should exceed those attained in the previous year. According to a Mr. Dyer, one of the last toll collectors, it was a 'killing job' in the winter when he may have collected just £2.10s.0d in a day, but this was compensated for by the unending stream of travellers heading to Devon and Cornwall during the summer months. The toll was 3d a vehicle in Mr. Dyer's day, when he paid £1,560 for the rights to levy tolls on passers-by. Out of any profit, £1,100 was paid in rates and taxes. The tolls were abolished in 1946 when the 5% bonds that financed the construction of the bridge were redeemed.

Refreshments In Burrowbridge, the Old Bakery is now a restaurant, whilst the King Alfred Inn serves meals and snacks.

Appendices

APPENDIX 1 — Routes in order of difficulty

As an experienced walker, I would class all of the walks in this book as easy if I were tackling them on my own. However, these are Family Walks and the grading should be read with this in mind. They apply to a fairly active seven or eight year old, rather than a hardened veteran!

Easy Walks:

Route   1 — *Nettlebridge and Harridge Wood.*
Route   2 — *Charterhouse and Velvet Bottom.*
Route   5 — *Compton Bishop and Crook Peak.*
Route   8 — *Around Brent Knoll.*
Route   9 — *Westhay Moor and the River Brue.*
Route 10 — *Glastonbury and the Tor.*

Moderately Difficult:

Route   3 — *Priddy Mineries and North Hill.*
Route   7 — *Around North Wotton.*
Route 11 — *Baltonsborough and the River Brue.*
Route 12 — *Huntspill and Bridgwater Bay.*
Route 13 — *Moorlinch and the Polden Hills.*
Route 14 — *Westonzoyland and Kings Sedgemoor Drain.*
Route 16 — *Burrow Mump and Southlake Moor.*

More Strenuous:

Route   4 — *Cheddar and the Gorge.*
Route   6 — *Wookey Hole and Ebbor Gorge.*
Route 15 — *Around High Ham.*

APPENDIX 2 — Bus Operators in the Area

Badgerline Buses .... Tel. Bath 464446
Tel. Bristol 297979
Tel. Weston-super-Mare 621201
Tel. Wells 73084
Southern National Ltd. .... Tel. Taunton 72033
Yeovil 76233

APPENDIX 3 — Tourist Information Centres in the Area

Bridgwater	Town Hall, High Street	Tel. Bridgwater 427652
Burnham-on-Sea	Berrow Road	Tel. Burnham 787852
Cheddar	Cheddar Library, Union Street	Tel. Cheddar 742769
Frome	Cattle Market Car Park	Tel. Frome 67271
Glastonbury	1 Marchant Buildings, Northload Street	Tel. Glastonbury 32954
Shepton Mallet	Petticoat Lane	Tel. S. Mallet 5258
Taunton	The Library, Corporation St.	Tel. Taunton 274785
Wells	Town Hall, Market Place	Tel. Wells 72552
Yeovil	Petters House, Petters Way	Tel. Yeovil 71279

APPENDIX 4 — 1:25,000 Pathfinder Sheets Used in Preparing the Walks

The 1:25,000 sheets are based upon a scale of 2½ inches to the mile. Their great advantage is in showing field boundaries and in pinpointing the actual right-of-way. These are in a sense your passport to be crossing what might otherwise appear to be private farmland!

Route 1 — *ST 64/74 Frome and Shepton Mallet*
Route 2 — *ST 45/55 Cheddar*
Route 3 — *ST 45/55 Cheddar*
Route 4 — *ST 45/55 Cheddar*
Route 5 — *1197 Brent Knoll*
Route 6 — *ST 44/54 Wells and Wedmore*
Route 7 — *ST 44/54 Wells and Wedmore*
Route 8 — *1197 Brent Knoll*
Route 9 — *ST 44/54 Wells and Wedmore*
Route 10 — *ST 43/53 Glastonbury and Street*
Route 11 — *ST 43/53 Glastonbury and Street*
Route 12 — *ST 24/34 Burnham-on-Sea*
Route 13 — *ST 23/33 Bridgwater*
Route 14 — *ST 23/33 Bridgwater*
Route 15 — *ST 43/53 Glastonbury and Street*
Route 16 — *ST 22/32 Taunton*
                ST 23/33 Bridgwater

APPENDIX 5 — Wet Weather Alternatives. Completely or partly under cover.

Museums and Art Galleries

Axbridge — King John's Hunting Lodge (N.T.). Merchant's house of around 1500. Local archaeology and geology. Open April-Sept. daily 2-5.

Bridgwater — Admiral Blake Museum. Relics of Blake's family and career. Battle of Sedgemoor. Local paintings and photos. Open Tues.-Sat. 11-4.

Cheddar — Gough's Cave Museum. Ancient artefacts found in the caves. Prehistoric scenes reconstructed. Open Easter-Sept. daily 10-6.

Glastonbury — Somerset Rural Life Museum. Displays plus occasional demonstrations of local crafts. Open daily 10-4.

Glastonbury — The Tribunal. Archaeology of the Somerset Levels including finds from the Lake Villages. Open Monday-Sat. 9-4.

Shepton Mallet Museum. Displays relating to local history. Open P.M. Monday-Friday.

Somerset County Museum, Taunton Castle. Extensive collection of local displays. Open Monday-Friday 10-5 and Summer Saturdays.

Somerset Levels Museum, near Westhay. Small exhibition on the Peat Moors at the Willows Garden Centre. Open daily 9-5.

Street — Shoe Museum. History of an important local industry. Open Easter-October 10-5.

Wells Museum. Local archaeology including finds from Wookey Hole Caves. Open Monday-Saturday P.M.

Weston-super-Mare Woodspring Museum. Extensive local displays. Open Monday-Saturday 10-5.

Industrial Interest

East Somerset Railway — Cranmore. Portion of former Witham to Wells line, managed by artist David Shepherd. Open most weekends.

Taunton — British Telecom Museum. History of telecommunications. Open Sats. 1.30-5.

Westonzoyland Pumping Station. 1½ miles from Westonzoyland on the road to Burrowbridge. Steam pumping-engine used in draining Levels. Open first Sunday of month 2-5.

Wookey Hole Paper Mill. 17th-century paper mill. Part of caves complex. Open daily 10-4.

Yeovil — Fleet Air Arm Museum. Displays include Concorde 002 prototype. Open daily 10-5.30.

Historic Buildings

Downside Abbey. Large Catholic public-school near Shepton Mallet. Church open at any time. Abbey and School by arrangement.

Glastonbury Abbey. Open daily 9.30-sunset.

High Ham Windmill. Thatched windmill dating from the early 19th century. Open Sundays Easter-September 2-5.30.

Meare — Abbot's Fish House. 14th century house used to store salt and fish for Glastonbury Abbey. Open daily.

Nunney Castle — near Frome. Open daily during daylight hours.

Wells Cathedral. England's first completely Gothic cathedral. Open daily.

Some other places of interest

Bradford-on-Tone — Sheppey's Farmhouse Cider. Press room, orchards, museum. Open April-Dec. Mon.-Sat. 8.30-dusk.

Cheddar Caves. Magnificent limestone formations deep underground. Open daily 10-4.

Chewton Mendip — Chewton Cheese Dairy. Demonstrations of cheese making twice each day. Open daily 10-4.

North Wootton Vineyard. 6-acre vineyard planted 1971. Open Mon.-Sat. 10-5.

Pilton Manor Vineyard. Making of "Moselle type" wines. Open Wed.-Fri. during summer months.

Wookey Hole Caves. More limestone caverns and formations. Additional attractions include waxworks, paper-making and penny arcade. Open daily 10-4.

* It is important to check opening times with either the attraction itself or the nearest Tourist Information Centre since such times are often subject to change. The Tourist Information Centres can also advise on attractions such as swimming pools and leisure centres.

FAMILY WALKS SERIES

Family Walks in the Lake District. Barry McKay. ISBN 0 907758 40 1.

Family Walks in West Yorkshire. Howard Beck. ISBN 0 907758 43 6.

Family Walks in Three Peaks and Malham. Howard Beck. ISBN 0 907758 42 8.

Family Walks in South Yorkshire. Norman Taylor. ISBN 0 907758 25 8.

Family Walks in Cheshire. Chris Buckland. ISBN 0 907758 29 0.

Family Walks in the Staffordshire Peak and Potters. Les Lumsdon. ISBN 0 907758 34 7.

Family Walks in the White Peak. Norman Taylor. ISBN 0 907758 09 6.

Family Walks in the Dark Peak. Norman Taylor. ISBN 0 907758 16 9.
Family Walks in Snowdonia. Laurence Main. ISBN 0 907758 32 0.

Family Walks in Mid Wales. Laurence Main. ISBN 0 907758 27 4.

Family Walks in South Shropshire. Marian Newton. ISBN 0 907758 30 4.

Family Walks in the Teme Valley. Camilla Harrison. ISBN 0 907758 45 2.

Family Walks in Hereford and Worcester. Gordon Ottewell. ISBN 0 907758 20 7.

Family Walks in the Wye Valley. Heather and Jon Hurley. ISBN 0 907758 26 6.

Family Walks in the Cotswolds. Gordon Ottewell. ISBN 0 907758 15 0.

Family Walks in South Gloucestershire. Gordon Ottewell. ISBN 0 907758 33 9.

Family Walks in Oxfordshire. Laurence Main. ISBN 0 907758 38 X.

Family Walks around Bristol, Bath and the Mendips. Nigel Vile. ISBN 0 907758 19 3.

Family Walks in Wiltshire. Nigel Vile. ISBN 0 907758 21 5.

Family Walks in Berkshire and North Hampshire. Kathy Sharp. ISBN 0 907758 37 1.

Family Walks on Exmoor and the Quantocks John Caswell. ISBN 0 907758 46 0.

Family Walks in Mendip, Avalon and Sedgemoor. Nigel Vile. ISBN 0 907758 41 X.

Family Walks in North West Kent. Clive Cutter. ISBN 0 907758 36 3.

Ready Spring 1992

Family Walks in the Weald of Kent and Sussex
Family Walks in North Yorkshire
Family Walks around Luton and Dunstable
Family Walks in Northumbria
Family Walks in Nottinghamshire
Family Walks on the Isle of Wight
Family Walks in Clwyd
Family Walks in Dorset
Family Walks in Rossendale, Pendle and Bowland

Other titles under consideration

The Publishers, D. J. Mitchell and E. G. Power welcome suggestions for further titles in this Series; and will be pleased to consider other manuscripts of Derbyshire and regional interest from new or established authors.
